Trades, Jumps, and Stops

MW01102421

Early Algebra

Catherine Twomey Fosnot
Patricia Lent

*first*hand
An imprint of Heinemann
A division of Reed Elsevier Inc.
361 Hanover Street
Portsmouth, NH 03801–3912
firsthand.heinemann.com

Harcourt School Publishers
6277 Sea Harbor Drive
Orlando, FL 32887–6777
www.harcourtschool.com

Offices and agents throughout the world

ISBN 13: 978-0-325-01015-1
ISBN 10: 0-325-01015-3

ISBN 13: 978-0-15-360567-3
ISBN 10: 0-15-360567-7

© 2007 Catherine Twomey Fosnot

The development of a portion of the material described within was supported in part by the National Science Foundation under Grant No. 9911841. Any opinions, findings, and conclusions or recommendations expressed in these materials are those of the authors and do not necessarily reflect the views of the National Science Foundation.

Library of Congress Cataloging-in-Publication Data
CIP data is on file with the Library of Congress

Printed in the United States of America on acid-free paper

11 10 09 08 07   ML   1 2 3 4 5 6

Acknowledgements

Photography

Herbert Seignoret
Mathematics in the City, City College of New York

Illustrator

Terri Murphy

Schools featured in photographs

The Muscota New School/PS 314 (an empowerment school in Region 10), New York, NY
Independence School/PS 234 (Region 9), New York, NY
Fort River Elementary School, Amherst, MA

Contents

Unit Overview

The story context of *The Masloppy Family Goes to New York City* sets the stage in this unit for a series of investigations to develop several big ideas and strategies important in the algebra strand. Seven-year-old Nicholas Masloppy (fondly known as the Organizer) and his brother and sisters are all waiting for the very special night when the family's big piggy bank will be opened. The family has been saving for a long time and now the bank is full. They are hoping to have enough money to go to New York City, where they will ride the subway to the Empire State Building, take a boat ride around the city, and visit the American Museum of Natural History. When the bank is opened, Nicholas's task is to organize the money into three equivalent piles for the three excursions.

The piggy bank context is developed in the story and then used in the unit as an important model for exchange and equivalence. The coins in the bank cannot be distributed into three piles evenly because not all of the coins are in multiples of three. Children need to redistribute and exchange coins in order to make three equivalent amounts. As the unit progresses, the piggy bank context is used to introduce and analyze equations and to develop strategies for simplifying them, such as using the associative and commutative

The Landscape of Learning

BIG IDEAS

- ☀ Equivalence
- ☀ Numeric expressions as objects to be operated on
- ☀ Properties of commutativity and associativity for addition
- ☀ Net change
- ☀ Variables can be used to represent unknowns

STRATEGIES

- ☀ Using procedural arithmetic
- ☀ Using substitution
- ☀ Using equivalence to separate off amounts to simplify computation
- ☀ Using associativity and commutativity
- ☀ Operating on expressions: undoing
- ☀ Examining equations for cases in which $n = 0$
- ☀ Justifying by doing several problems
- ☀ Justifying by explaining why

MODEL

- ☀ Double open number line

properties, "canceling," and substituting. Variables are introduced with the additional context of foreign coins of unknown denominations.

As the unit progresses, the context of subway stops at which numbers of passengers board and detrain is used to explore net change and functions. Equivalent expressions are generated as ways to describe the changes and children work to develop convincing proofs that they have found all the possible ways.

Several minilessons for algebra are also included in the unit. These are structured initially as a game of "twenty questions" to determine the denominations of hidden coins totaling 50 cents and later as strings of related problems. Initially the focus of the minilessons is on equivalent trades and writing mathematical statements using the relational signs <, >, and =. As the unit progresses, the minilessons support the development of an understanding of the commutative and associative properties of addition, and of strategies for simplifying equations and solving for unknowns (focusing on strategies such as "canceling," substituting using equivalence, and undoing.)

The Mathematical Landscape

What is algebra and how does understanding of it develop? Algebra includes many aspects—for instance, generalizing beyond specific instances; describing and representing patterns and functions; building equations and expressions using symbolic representations with integers and variables; and manipulating symbols to simplify equations, prove relations, and solve for unknowns.

From 2003 to 2006, several mathematicians, researchers, and teachers participated in a think tank at Mathematics in the City to explore several questions:

• What might algebra look like as it emerges in the elementary years?

• What are some of the critical big ideas and strategies young learners construct that might serve as important landmarks for teachers to notice, develop, and celebrate?

• How might realistic contexts and models support such development?

To answer these questions, we designed instructional sequences and field-tested many activities. This unit and *The California Frog-Jumping Contest*, a fourth- and fifth-grade unit also in the *Contexts for Learning Mathematics* series, are a result of the work we did together.

The most commonly employed model for algebra, used to develop an understanding of equations, is the balance pan. But the use of this model can be complicated by the fact that children do not necessarily have a deep enough understanding of conservation of weight for this model to make sense (Piaget 1954). In our previous work on number and operation (addressed in many of the other units in the *Contexts for Learning Mathematics* series), we used the open number line model. Because our algebra work was an extension of children's work with arithmetic, we began to explore the use of the open number line as a model for algebra as well.

The open number line aligns better than base-ten blocks with children's invented strategies for addition and subtraction and it stimulates a mental representation of numbers and number operations that is more powerful for developing mental arithmetic strategies. Children using the open number line are cognitively involved in their actions. In contrast, children who use base-ten blocks or the hundred chart tend to depend primarily on visualization, which results in a passive "reading off" behavior rather than in cognitive involvement in the actions undertaken (Klein, Beishuizen, and Treffers 2002). We found the open number line was a very helpful model for algebra as well (Fosnot and Jacob, in preparation).

In contrast to a number line with counting numbers written below, an "open" number line is just an empty line used to record children's addition and subtraction strategies. Only the numbers children use are recorded and the addition and subtraction are recorded as leaps or jumps. For example, if a child's strategy for adding 8 + 79 is 79 + 1 + 7, using a landmark number of 80, it can be recorded like this:

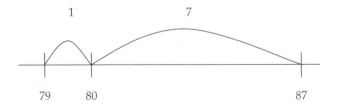

As we researched the development of big ideas and strategies in the algebra strand, we used a double open number line, with one expression represented above the line and the other represented underneath. In the following example from a second-grade classroom, children are analyzing the equation 8 + 6 = 9 + 5. They have been asked to consider whether it is a true statement or not.

Lily: True, because 9 is 1 more than 8 and 6 is 1 more than 5.

Trish (the teacher) records Lily's thinking on the double open number line:

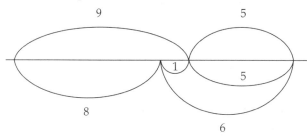

Sam: I don't get it.

Haille: It's like taking 1 from the 6 and giving it to the 8. You get 9 + 5 = 5 + 9.

Sam: Oh, cool.

Carmen: You could also do 10 + 4 = 4 + 10.

This model is a powerful tool in developing a deep understanding of equations. It supports children in exploring associativity and commutativity and in constructing rules for simplifying equations (such as "cancellation" and substitution). In the upper grades the model helps students develop strategies for solving simultaneous equations with two unknowns.

In this unit the double number line is introduced using the hands-on model of a string of connecting cubes. The string includes two different colors of cubes arranged in alternating groups of five cubes of each color (see page 10). The assumption is that your students have not had much experience with the open number line before this unit. If they have, you may prefer to bypass the hands-on model and go directly to the open number line. If you prefer to introduce the open number line first, please see the *Contexts for Learning Mathematics* unit *Measuring for the Art Show* where it is developed.

This unit is designed to encourage the development of some of the big ideas related to early algebra:

❖ *equivalence*

❖ *numeric expressions as objects to be operated on (in contrast to arithmetic procedures)*

❖ *properties of commutativity and associativity for addition*

❖ *net change*

❖ *variables can be used to represent unknowns*

❖ Equivalence

Equivalence—knowing that two expressions may be equivalent even though they don't look alike—is one of the most important ideas in early algebra. Equations are based on an understanding of equivalence. Young learners often think the equal sign means that "the answer is coming" (Carpenter, Franke, and Levi 2003), probably because many teachers tend to write equations as the result of arithmetic, with the answer on the right of the sign. Equations are much more than a representation of arithmetic. They are mathematical statements that represent an equivalent relationship between expressions. Early on in the development of mathematical understanding, children struggle to understand the statement $5 + 3 = 4 + 4$. The numbers are different, so how can the two sides be equal? At first, children need to add the numbers on each side to be certain. Eventually, as they construct the idea of compensation—in this case, that one is lost from the five but gained onto the three—they have less need to do the arithmetic. But this is just the beginning of the development of an understanding of equivalence. In grades two and three, equivalence is expanded to the analysis of statements like $8 + 2 + 10 = 12 + 4 + 4$, and it includes the generalization that equivalence is maintained no matter what operation you use on an equation, as long as you do it to both sides. Thus the statement $n + 8 + 2 + 10 = 12 + 4 + 4 + n$ is also true.

❖ Numeric expressions as objects to be operated on (in contrast to arithmetic procedures)

Initially children approach equations with arithmetic. They proceed with the necessary operations as they read, left to right. To analyze whether or not the statement $8 + 2 + 26 + 2 = 28 + 8 + 2$ is true, they do arithmetic step by step, starting with $8 + 2$, adding 26 next, and then adding 2. On the right side they start with 28, add 8, and then add 2, producing $38 = 38$. In contrast, when expressions are treated as objects that can be operated on, children can look at $8 + 2 + 26 + 2 = 28 + 8 + 2$ and quickly see that if some of the numbers are combined, for example $26 + 2$, the result is $8 + 2 + 28$ on each side. Alternatively, children might subtract 26 from each side and produce $8 + 2 + 2$ on each side. Done! No need for further arithmetic.

When students encounter expressions with variables in later years, one major difficulty is that they attempt to use arithmetic and when it doesn't work they don't know how to proceed. How do you solve $2x + 5 = 3x - 6$ with arithmetic if you don't know what x is? But when you understand that the expressions are objects and that amounts can be added to or subtracted from them and equivalence is maintained, you just add the number $-2x + 6$ to both sides, resulting in $11 = x$. Children do learn these procedures to solve for unknowns, but if they have not constructed the idea of expressions as objects that can be operated on, the procedures are only rote and without meaning.

❖ Properties of commutativity and associativity for addition

Algebraically, commutativity can be represented as $a + b = b + a$, and associativity as $(a + b) + c = a + (b + c)$. Children need many opportunities to compose and decompose numbers before they come to realize that numbers can be grouped in a variety of ways, even turned around, and the amounts stay the same. These properties do not hold for subtraction, and children can be amazed and puzzled as they explore this difference.

❖ Net change

Exploring patterns of change and generalizing across situations is what net change is about, and it is this big idea that underlies the early development of functions. Think about an input/output situation in which, no matter what number you put in, what comes out is always two less than the initial number. Or consider a subway: a number of people on the train get off at a stop, and new passengers get on. When the train takes off again, there are two fewer people than before. Now think about all the possible numbers of people involved. No matter how many people get off the train, the number of people boarding is always two less than the number who detrain. Being able to generalize and characterize net gain or loss across situations is an important big idea for young learners.

❖ Variables can be used to represent unknowns

A variable is a number that may have different values. Examine the statement $n + 3 = 3 + n$. Since $3 = 3$, n can be any number and the equality still holds. Understanding a variable as a number that can have one or many values is a difficult concept for children to construct, because they must generalize. Initially they think of a variable as a secret number with a specific value, and it is difficult for them to realize that it may have several values. Variables have often been introduced to young learners as missing addends: $8 + n = 10$. This is not difficult for children to figure out; they usually just count on from 8. But this type of introduction to variables can cause many problems later on, because it only affirms the child's idea of a variable as a secret number having one and only one value. In this unit, variables are explored both ways: in situations in which they have many values and as unknowns with a specific value.

As you work with the activities in this unit, you will observe children using many strategies to derive answers. Here are some strategies to notice:

- *using procedural arithmetic*
- *using substitution*
- *using equivalence to separate off amounts to simplify computation*
- *using associativity and commutativity*
- *operating on expressions: undoing*
- *examining equations for cases in which n = 0*
- *justifying by doing several problems*
- *justifying by explaining why*

❖ *Using procedural arithmetic*

As mentioned earlier, children initially approach equations with arithmetic. They proceed as they read, left to right. To analyze whether or not the statement $8 + 2 + 26 + 2 = 28 + 8 + 2$ is true, they do arithmetic step by step, starting with $8 + 2$ and adding 26 and then 2. On the other side of the equal sign they start with 28 and add 8 and then 2, producing $38 = 38$. This is an early strategy that will probably be abandoned once children construct an understanding of several of the big ideas and strategies developed in this unit.

❖ *Using substitution*

Once children understand equivalence, they will begin to substitute one expression for another. For example, to subtract 5, a child might add 5 and then subtract 10. Or a child might solve $32 + 38$ by substituting the equivalent expression of $30 + 40$.

❖ *Using equivalence to separate off amounts to simplify computation*

As understanding of equations increases, a child may begin to simplify them by eliminating quantities that are on both sides of the equal sign. For example, in the statement $8 + 2 + 26 + 2 = 28 + 8 + 2$, the $8 + 2$ can be "canceled" on each side to produce $26 + 2 = 28$. At first children are reluctant to "cancel:" they draw lines through the identical numbers on each side of the equal sign but won't erase them, or they talk about ignoring those numbers momentarily. As they become more confident that the equivalence remains, they develop what they often call a "cross-out" rule.

❖ *Using associativity and commutativity*

The problem $19 + 32 + 8 = ?$ can be solved by adding 19 and 32 first. But the problem can be made a bit easier to solve by grouping the 32 and 8 first: $(19 + 32) + 8 = 19 + (32 + 8)$. Children may understand that they can group numbers in addition without changing the total sum, but they often don't think to use this strategy. Besides being an important big idea, the associative property of addition is also an important strategy to encourage. The strategy can be very helpful in simplifying equations because the grouping may allow for "canceling" of equivalent expressions on each side of the equal sign. The same can be said for commutativity. When analyzing the statement $8 + 15 + 3 + 2 = 15 + 8 + 5$, the use of a combination of the associative and commutative properties allows children to conclude that the statement is true without doing all of the arithmetic to derive $28 = 28$.

❖ *Operating on expressions: undoing*

Once children are confident that quantities can be "canceled" and that adding or subtracting identical quantities on each side of an equation won't disturb equivalence, they begin to operate with addition and subtraction as a strategy to simplify equations. They develop an undoing strategy. For example, they might add 6 to each side of an equation to get rid of −6, or subtract 6 from each side to get rid of +6.

❖ *Examining equations for cases in which n = 0*

As children begin to understand that adding a number n to both sides of an equation does not disturb equivalence, they often overgeneralize and assume that if n is on only one side of the equation the statement is untrue. For example, consider the following:

$$4 + 8 + 12 = 12 + 12 + n$$

Initially children may argue that this is not a true statement since n is on only one side. Soon they come to realize that the statement is true if and only if $n = 0$, and they begin to realize the importance of examining for this case.

❖ Justifying by doing several problems

Initially children think that "proving" means to try something out several times. When asked how they know their strategy will always work, they justify their claim by showing how the strategy worked several times, and they just keep giving additional examples.

❖ Justifying by explaining why

One of the first major developments in children's thinking is realizing that merely showing several examples is not a sufficient justification. They realize that they can never rule out the possibility that it won't work in some other example, and they can't try out infinite numbers of possibilities. At this point children begin to recognize that a justification based on the reasoning behind the strategy may be more convincing and more generalizable.

MATHEMATICAL MODELING

The model used in this unit is the double open number line. Models go through three stages of development (Gravemeijer 1999; Fosnot and Dolk 2001):

- ❖ *model of the situation*
- ❖ *model of children's strategies*
- ❖ *model as a tool for thinking*

❖ Model of the situation

Initially models grow out of modeling the situation—in this unit, a string of connecting cubes is used to explore equivalence. The string includes two different colors of cubes arranged in alternating groups of five cubes of each color.

❖ Model of children's strategies

Children benefit from having teachers model their strategies. Once a model has been introduced as a representation of the situation, you can use it to depict children's strategies as they explain their thinking. For example, in analyzing the equation $5 + 4 + 10 = 10 + 5 + 5$, some children may just compare the $5 + 5$ to $5 + 4$. This can be represented on the double number line in several ways, depending on what a particular child says. For example, if a child

says, "I knew the tens were the same, and 5 plus 4 is 1 less than 5 plus 5," you can draw the following:

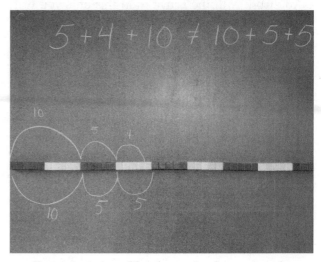

Representations like these give learners a chance to discuss and envision each other's strategies.

❖ Model as a tool for thinking

Eventually children become able to use the model as a tool to think with—to explore and prove their ideas about equivalent relations and equivalent expressions that they might substitute in order to make computation easier.

Many opportunities to discuss these landmarks in mathematical development will arise as you work through this unit. Look for moments of puzzlement. Don't hesitate to let children discuss their ideas and check and recheck their strategies. Celebrate their accomplishments—they are young mathematicians at work!

A graphic of the full landscape of learning for early algebra is provided on page 12. The purpose of the graphic is to allow you to see the longer journey of children's mathematical development and to place your work with this unit within the scope of this long-term development. You may also find it helpful to use this graphic as a way to record the progress of individual children for yourself. Each landmark can be shaded in as you find evidence in a child's work and in what the child says—evidence that a landmark strategy, big idea, or way of modeling has been constructed. In a sense you will be recording the individual pathways your students take as they develop as young mathematicians!

Research Connections

An excellent summary of research and issues in the teaching and learning of algebra can be found in the chapter, "Developing Mathematical Proficiency Beyond Number" in *Adding It Up: Helping Children Learn Mathematics* (National Research Council 2001).

A thorough research-based overview of many of the cognitive issues in the learning of algebra can be found in the chapter, "The Learning and Teaching of School Algebra" in *The Handbook of Research on Mathematics Teaching and Learning* (Kieran 1992).

For a discussion of pre-algebraic strategies and the conceptual development of children's use of variables we recommend the chapter, "Equations with Multiple Variables and Repeated Variables" in *Thinking Mathematically: Integrating Arithmetic & Algebra in Elementary School* (Carpenter, Franke, Levi 2003). This book also discusses the development of the concept of equality and relational thinking at grades earlier than those for which this unit is recommended.

For discussion of the use of the open number line as a representational tool in understanding number and operation see *Young Mathematicians at Work: Constructing Number Sense, Addition, and Subtraction* (Fosnot and Dolk 2001).

References and Resources

Carpenter, Thomas P., Megan Loef Franke, and Linda Levi. 2003. *Thinking Mathematically: Integrating Arithmetic & Algebra in Elementary School.* Portsmouth, NH: Heinemann

Dolk, Maarten and Catherine Twomey Fosnot. 2004. *Working with the Number Line, Grades PreK–3: Mathematical Models.* CD-ROM with accompanying facilitator's guide by Antonia Cameron, Sherrin B. Hersch, and Catherine Twomey Fosnot. Portsmouth, NH: Heinemann.

Fosnot, Catherine Twomey, and Maarten Dolk. 2001. *Young Mathematicians at Work: Constructing Number Sense, Addition, and Subtraction.* Portsmouth, NH: Heinemann.

Fosnot, Catherine Twomey, and Bill Jacob. In preparation. Young Mathematicians at Work: The Role of Contexts and Models in the Emergence of Proof. In *Teaching and Learning Proof Across the Grades,* eds. Despina Styliano, Marie Blanton, and Eric Knuth. Mahwah, NJ: Lawrence Erlbaum Associates, Inc.

Gravemeijer, Koeno. 1999. How emergent models may foster the constitution of formal mathematics. *Mathematical Thinking and Learning,* 1(2), 155–77.

Kieran, Carolyn. 1992. The learning and teaching of school algebra. In *The Handbook of Research on Mathematics Teaching and Learning,* ed. Douglas Grouws. New York, NY: Macmillan

Klein, Anton S., Meindert Beishuizen, and Adri Treffers. 2002. The empty number line in Dutch second grade. In *Lessons Learned from Research,* eds. Judith Sowder and Bonnie Schapelle. Reston, VA: National Council of Teachers of Mathematics.

National Research Council. 2001. *Adding It Up: Helping Children Learn Mathematics.* Washington, DC: National Academy Press.

Piaget, Jean. 1954. *The Construction of Reality in the Child.* London: Routledge and Kegan Paul.

Woodard, Mark. 2000. Mathematical Quotation Server: math.furman.edu/~mwoodard/mqs/mquot.shtml

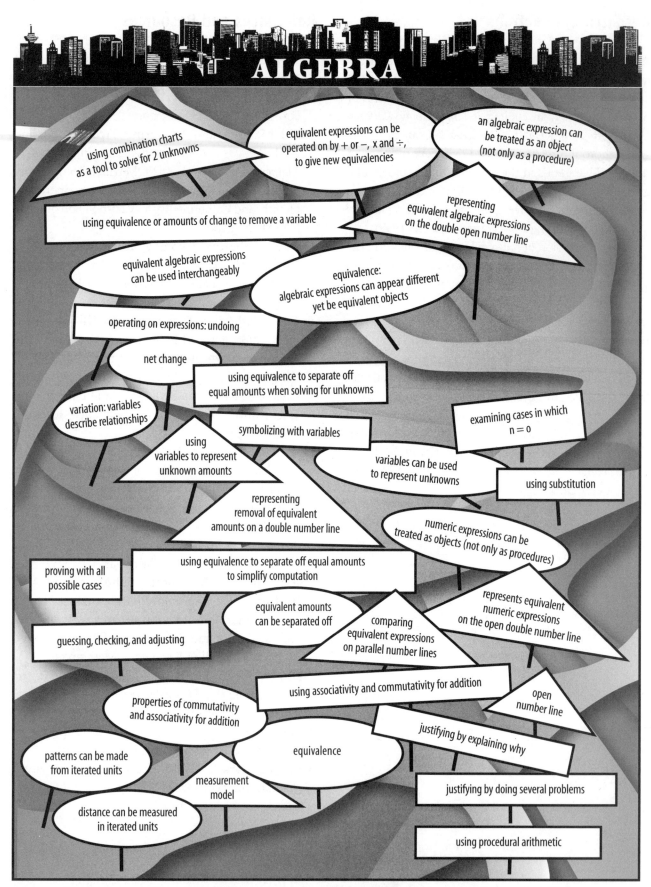

using combination charts
as a tool to solve for 2 unknowns

equivalent expressions can be
operated on by + or −, × and ÷,
to give new equivalencies

an algebraic expression can
be treated as an object
(not only as a procedure)

using equivalence or amounts of change to remove a variable

representing
equivalent algebraic expressions
on the double open number line

equivalent algebraic expressions
can be used interchangeably

equivalence:
algebraic expressions can appear different
yet be equivalent objects

operating on expressions: undoing

net change

using equivalence to separate off
equal amounts when solving for unknowns

variation: variables
describe relationships

symbolizing with variables

examining cases in which
$n = 0$

using
variables to represent
unknown amounts

variables can be used
to represent unknowns

using substitution

representing
removal of equivalent
amounts on a double number line

numeric expressions can be
treated as objects (not only as procedures)

proving with all
possible cases

using equivalence to separate off equal amounts
to simplify computation

represents equivalent
numeric expressions
on the open double number line

equivalent amounts
can be separated off

comparing
equivalent expressions
on parallel number lines

guessing, checking, and adjusting

using associativity and commutativity for addition

open
number line

properties of commutativity
and associativity for addition

justifying by explaining why

patterns can be made
from iterated units

equivalence

measurement
model

justifying by doing several problems

distance can be measured
in iterated units

using procedural arithmetic

The landscape of learning: algebra on the horizon showing landmark strategies (rectangles), big ideas (ovals), and models (triangles).

DAY ONE

The Masloppy Family Goes to New York City

The context of fair-sharing coins into three equivalent amounts is developed with the story *The Masloppy Family Goes to New York City*. After hearing you read the story, children work in pairs to determine how to group the coins into three equivalent amounts. A subsequent math congress provides an opportunity for discussion of strategies, with emphasis on the ideas of exchange and equivalence.

Day One Outline

Developing the Context

☀ Read *The Masloppy Family Goes to New York City* up to the point when the coins are being rolled. Ask the children to discuss how many coins go in a roll and record their ideas with equations.

☀ Finish the story and ask children to figure out what coins Nicholas put in each bag.

Supporting the Investigation

☀ Support and challenge the children to group the coins into three equivalent amounts.

Preparing for the Math Congress

☀ Take note of the strategies the children are using.

☀ Do not encourage them to determine the total value of the coins. Instead, focus on how some coins can be substituted for others.

☀ Plan for a math congress discussion on the ideas of substitution and equivalence.

Facilitating the Math Congress

☀ Begin the congress with a discussion of a distributing strategy and then move to a discussion of substitution.

☀ Record children's solutions and discuss whether or not the solutions work.

Materials Needed

The Masloppy Family Goes to New York City [If you do not have the full-color read-aloud book (available from Heinemann), you can use Appendix A.]

Small plastic bag containing empty coin wrappers (three nickel wrappers, six quarter wrappers, three dime wrappers, three penny wrappers) and some coins (four quarters, one dime, seven nickels, and five pennies)—one bag per pair of children

Student recording sheet for the coins investigation (Appendix B)—one per pair of children

Before class, prepare an overhead transparency of Appendix B.

Overhead projector

Large chart pad and easel (or chalkboard or whiteboard)

Markers

Developing the Context

☀ Read *The Masloppy Family Goes to New York City* up to the point when the coins are being rolled. Ask the children to discuss how many coins go in a roll and record their ideas with equations.

☀ Finish the story and ask children to figure out what coins Nicholas put in each bag.

Read the story aloud. When you come to the part in which the coins are being rolled and Nicholas and Delia are figuring out how many coins go in a roll, encourage the children to discuss their ideas. Record their ideas with equations where appropriate, using the equal sign. For example, if a child says 4 quarters make 1 dollar, 20 quarters make 5 dollars, and 20 plus 20 equals 40 and 5 plus 5 equals 10, you might explain that you will draw coins and write the amounts. You would then write something like the following:

$$4\,\textcircled{25} = \$1$$

$$4\,\textcircled{25} + 4\,\textcircled{25} + 4\,\textcircled{25} + 4\,\textcircled{25} + 4\,\textcircled{25} = \$1 + \$1 + \$1 + \$1 + \$1$$

$$20\,\textcircled{25} = \$5$$

$$20\,\textcircled{25} + 20\,\textcircled{25} = \$5 + \$5$$

$$40\,\textcircled{25} = \$10$$

When you have finished reading the story, suggest that the children work on figuring out what coins Nicholas put in each bag. Remind them that the value of the money in each of the three bags is equivalent. Assign math partners and distribute a recording sheet (Appendix B) and a plastic bag containing the wrappers and coins to each pair of children.

Behind the Numbers

Empty wrappers (rather than rolls of coins) are used so that children will not have large amounts of money to deal with. The numbers of wrappers (six and three) have been carefully chosen to encourage children to distribute the wrappers into three piles. The real problem then lies in finding ways to distribute the loose coins (which add up to $1.50) equally. If children begin by distributing the wrappers into three equal piles, they will probably do the same with the four loose quarters, the seven nickels, and the five pennies. This will produce the problem of what to do with the remaining quarter, dime, nickel, and two pennies. This impossible situation will require children to exchange equivalent amounts as they attempt to redistribute the coins, for example using five nickels for the boat trip; a dime, two nickels, and five pennies for the museum trip; and a quarter for the subway trip. Other combinations are possible as well. Do not allow children to exchange for other coins from the class box of coins. Only the coins in the plastic bags may be used. This constraint pushes children to think about equivalence and to exchange and substitute equivalent amounts. If children request other coins, stay grounded in the context by reminding them that these are the exact coins that Nicholas had.

Supporting the Investigation

As children work, walk around and take note of the strategies you see. Confer as needed to support and challenge their investigation.

Conferring with Children at Work

Inside One Classroom

Jasmine: I think we need to add up all this money, first.

Keshawn: That's a lot of money. Two, 4, 6. Six dollars for the nickels. Write that down. Six rolls of quarters—10, 20…60. Sixty dollars in quarters. Wow. That's a lot of quarters!

Trish (the teacher): It is, isn't it! I wonder if we need to add all this up. Could we divide it up without adding it all up?

Jasmine: I could pass out the wrappers. One, two, three… One, two, three…

Trish: Passing everything out to three piles—that's a great idea. I'll check back with you in a little bit.

Author's Notes

During the investigation, Trish will probably have time to sit and confer with only four or five pairs of children. She also moves around the room noting the kinds of strategies that children are using. Children can work autonomously and they are learning even when she is not there because they are discussing and reflecting in pairs.

By pondering aloud whether the addition is needed, Trish invites a consideration of an alternative strategy. She does not suggest that the wrappers be divided up; she only wonders aloud if another way is possible. She respects the children's autonomy and trusts them to generate clever solutions.

Preparing for the Math Congress

As you move around the room, take note of the various strategies being used. Here are some strategies you might see:

❖ Adding up the amounts first to get a total of $84 and then struggling to figure out how to divide this amount into three equivalent piles.

❖ Distributing the wrappers first and then continuing to distribute the coins. This strategy results in a remaining quarter, dime, nickel, and two pennies—a situation that will require undoing the initial distribution of the coins and searching for equivalent amounts to exchange, such as a dime and three nickels for a quarter. Here the strategy may become characteristic of trial and error as children search for ways to make three equivalent amounts. You may see counting and adding strategies or systematic substitution, for example, two nickels for a dime, or five nickels for a quarter, etc.

❖ Distributing the wrappers but adding up the coins, and realizing that since the total amount in coins is $1.50, each bag needs 50 cents. As children search for ways to make 50 cents, you may see adding of the amounts and then counting to see if the amounts are equivalent. Or you may see the use of systematic grouping as children add (for example, two nickels for a dime or five nickels for a quarter.)

❖ Realizing that more than one possibility exists and making a list of some possibilities.

It is not important that children realize that the coins add up to $1.50 and that each bag needs 50 cents. Do not encourage them to determine the total value of the coins. It is the equivalency and the exchange that is important. In fact, calculating the total and then just finding ways to make 50 cents can become a simple addition exercise, with the result being that the algebraic thinking is sacrificed. Focus on how some coins can be substituted for others. Even if children do not find a solution, the exchanging they are doing as they investigate is important for the development of algebraic thinking.

■ Tips for Structuring the Math Congress

Several big ideas about algebra are likely to have emerged in this investigation: equivalence and substitution (exchange); the generalization that a substitution strategy allows for several possibilities to exist; and the idea that the wrappers are not important because each bag has the same number, so the most important part of the problem is how to distribute the coins to make equivalent amounts. You will want to make these ideas the focus of the math congress.

Facilitating the Math Congress

☀ Begin the congress with a discussion of a distributing strategy and then move to a discussion of substitution.

☀ Record children's solutions and discuss whether or not the solutions work.

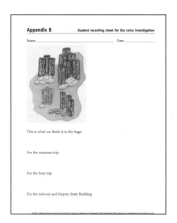

Convene the children in the meeting area to discuss their strategies. Have them sit next to their partners with their recording sheets. Display the overhead transparency of Appendix B and start the congress with a discussion of distributing the wrappers and the loose coins first. Have someone share who utilized the distributing strategy and then struggled with what to do with the remaining coins that could not be distributed equally.

Establish that each pile had two quarter wrappers and one each of nickel, dime, and penny wrappers. Ask if anyone solved the dilemma of what to do with the loose coins and choose (to share next) a pair of children who began to substitute (exchange) equivalent amounts by trial and error. Write down the equivalent expressions they mention, such as 5(5)= 1(25) or 1(10) + 3(5) = 1(25). Make sure that everyone agrees that the amounts of money exchanged are equivalent. Once the equivalency and the idea of trading are established, ask for solutions that worked and write them down on chart paper. For example:

Museum trip: Wrappers + 1(10) + 7(5) + 5(1)

Boat trip: Wrappers + 2(25)

Subway ride and Empire State Building trip: Wrappers + 2(25)

Ask the community to consider if this solution works. Lay out the coins and have children physically exchange them to prove the equivalency. Explore other solutions and establish the equivalency of each group of coins.

A Portion of the Math Congress

Author's Notes

Trish (the teacher): Ian, would you and Peter begin? Tell us what you did.

Ian: We shared out all the wrappers first. That was easy. Then we shared out the coins. We gave every pile a quarter. Then we did 2 nickels each. Last we did the pennies. But then we had this left over. *(Shows one quarter, one dime, one nickel, and two pennies.)* We're stuck. It's hard.

By starting with children who distributed and then were puzzled about what to do next, Trish frames the main problem that will engender the strategy of substitution and a discussion of equivalence.

Trish: This is tough, isn't it? I wonder what Nicholas, the Organizer, did. Does anybody have an idea that would help? It seems that sharing the wrappers was the easy part. I guess we don't have to worry now about the wrappers. We can work on the coins. Does anyone have a way to solve this?

Acknowledging that the problem is difficult allows the children to feel comfortable in admitting they aren't sure what to do. It also allows them to take risks and to work as a community to help each other.

Jasmine: I do. You can trade. Put a dime for 2 nickels. Then we can give two piles another nickel and the other pile can have 5 pennies. That's fair.

By commenting on the wrappers, Trish challenges the children to consider how equivalent amounts can momentarily be disregarded. Over time this will result in a "canceling" strategy. For now, the emphasis is on proving equivalence.

Trish: Turn to the person next to you and discuss what Jasmine did. Is this fair?

By asking for pair talk, Trish engages all the children in considering the strategy, and she pushes them to explain the exchange.

Amirah: Yes. We agree. But we still have a quarter and a nickel left. What do we do with those?

Trish: Did anyone find a way that worked? Is there a different exchange we could do?

By exploring alternative solutions, Trish establishes that there are other possibilities and encourages the children to inquire further.

Carmen: We found a way. José and I gave 2 quarters for one pile, and 2 quarters for another. Then the third pile had all of the other coins.

Trish: Let me write that down so we can all consider it. *(Writes:)* What do you think? Does this work?

Sally: It works! Seven nickels and 5 pennies and 1 dime is the same as 2 quarters! Each bag has wrappers and 50 cents!

Wrappers + 2 (25) = Wrappers + 2 (25) = Wrappers + 7 (5) + 5 (1) + 1 (10)

Marcus: Yep. And there's another way, too.

Trish: Another way, too? Let's check out your way, too. I wonder how many ways there are for Nicholas to do this?

An important part of algebra is generalizing and proving that all possibilities have been found.

Assessment Tips

Notice which children were comfortable trading and establishing equivalency and which needed to count or add to be sure. It is helpful to jot down your observations on sticky notes. These can be attached to children's recording sheets later and placed in their portfolios.

Differentiating Instruction

By allowing children to mathematize this fair-sharing situation in their own ways, you can be confident that you are differentiating appropriately. As the math congress progresses, though, be alert for moments when you can stretch and challenge children's thinking, as well as the important moments when you need to pull particular children into the discussion to be sure that they are following it. Use the context to help children realize the meaning of what they are doing. Talk about Nicholas and the coins in the piggy bank. Allow children to physically trade coins and check the results. For those children you want to challenge, encourage them to find all the possible combinations and to work toward proving that they have found them all.

Reflections on the Day

Today children were introduced to the context of fair-sharing money to explore equivalence. They developed strategies such as substituting and momentarily disregarding amounts already established to be equivalent as they explored representing the situation with equations. This early work with equivalence sets the stage for establishing the use of equivalent expressions and for analyzing equations.

The Piggy Bank

The day begins with a minilesson—"twenty questions" to determine the coins hidden in your hand. Then children learn a new game, Piggy Bank, which provides a context for building equations and offers further opportunities for exploring the ideas of equivalence and substitution.

Day Two Outline

Minilesson: "Twenty Questions" for Fifty Cents

☀ Ask children to share the thinking underlying their questions as they try to determine the value of the coins hidden in your hand.

☀ Record the solutions in equation form and ask children to discuss the possible exchanges made as you went from Problem #1 to Problem #2.

Developing the Context

☀ Model how to play Piggy Bank.

Supporting the Investigation

☀ As children play the game, encourage them to look for equivalence, rather than using arithmetic.

Materials Needed

Coins for the minilesson (one quarter, two dimes, four nickels, and fifteen pennies)

Bag of coins (quarters, nickels, dimes, and pennies)—one bag per pair of children

Piggy Bank game cards (Appendix C)— one deck per pair of children

Piggy Bank game board (Appendix D)— one per child

Student recording sheet for Piggy Bank (Appendix E)— one per pair of children

Large chart pad and easel

Markers

Minilesson: "Twenty Questions" for Fifty Cents
(10–15 minutes)

☀ Ask children to share the thinking underlying their questions as they try to determine the value of the coins hidden in your hand.

☀ Record the solutions in equation form and ask children to discuss the possible exchanges made as you went from Problem #1 to Problem #2.

Behind the Numbers

The coins have been chosen to encourage children to consider exchanges and equivalence. Problem #1 has no quarters and ten pennies. Notice whether children ask about pennies in multiples of five. Those who ask if you have six pennies, or two, are not yet able to understand that these numbers of coins are impossible given the total is 50 cents. Problem #2 encourages children to realize that even though the total is the same as in the first problem, the coins are different. When the equation is written at the end, children will need to discuss what coins you must have exchanged. Here there are a variety of possibilities. Do not explain what you did. Instead, challenge children to consider different possibilities and to search for all of them.

Note: If you have a linguistically diverse classroom or many ELL students, you may need to explicitly discuss different wording in the questions. For example, the difference between "Do you have a quarter?" and "Do you have one quarter?" may need some elaboration.

☀ Model how to play Piggy Bank.

This mental math minilesson uses the format of "twenty questions" to provide children with opportunities to think about equivalence. There are two problems; each uses coins totaling 50 cents. Place the coins in your closed palm without allowing children to identify them. Announce the total value of the coins (50 cents) in your hand. Have children take turns asking questions that can be answered only by yes or no, such as "Do you have a quarter?" or "Do you have two dimes?" (If you have only one dime in your hand, the answer would be no; if the question is "Do you have any dimes?" the answer would be yes.) Record the questions and answers on chart paper or the chalkboard as you proceed. Keep track of the number of questions it takes for the class to determine the exact coins you're holding. As you progress, notice children who are beginning to ask questions based on anticipating equivalence; for example, if the target is 50 cents and pennies and nickels have been ruled out, only two possibilities exist: two quarters or five dimes. Have children share the thinking underlying their questions.

Problem #1: 2 dimes, 10 pennies, 4 nickels (50 cents)
Problem #2: 15 pennies, 2 nickels, 1 quarter (50 cents)

After the two problems have been solved, write them in an equation form:

Equation: $2 ⑩ + 10 ① + 4 ⑤ = 15 ① + 2 ⑤ + 1 ㉕$

Then ask children to discuss what exchanges they think you made as you went from Problem #1 to Problem #2.

Developing the Context

Have the children sit in a circle in the meeting area. Play Piggy Bank with one child in the center of the circle as a way to introduce the game and model how it is played.

■ Object of the Game

The purpose of the game is to provide opportunities to write mathematical statements using the relational signs <, >, and =, and also to encourage children to examine equivalency without doing arithmetic to determine the totals.

Directions for Playing Piggy Bank

Children play the game in pairs. Each pair of children has a bag of coins, a deck of Piggy Bank game cards (Appendix C), and a recording sheet (Appendix E). Each individual player also has a Piggy Bank game board (Appendix D).

Children take turns selecting a card from the Piggy Bank deck. The card determines the amount they can place on their board. Players determine which coins to take. For example if a "15 cents" card is drawn, the player can take fifteen pennies, or a dime and a nickel, or three nickels, etc. The choice of coins is then placed on the player's board and recorded on the recording sheet.

Then Player Two chooses a card and places that amount on the other board, recording the transaction on the recording sheet. Both expressions are now on the same recording sheet and players need to determine which symbol to use: <, >, or =. If children are not familiar with the greater-than and

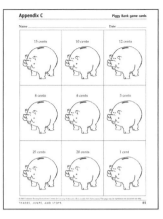

Quarter	Dimes	Nickels	Pennies

Quarter	Dimes	Nickels	Pennies

Sample game boards

less-than symbols, explain that the symbol always points to the smaller amount. Play continues as children add coins to the boards as determined by the cards drawn. For example, two boards are shown above.

The equation for these two game boards on the recording sheet would be:

$$1\,(25) + 2\,(10) + 8\,(1) = 4\,(10) + 1\,(5) + 8\,(1)$$

In this case, the equal sign would be used. As you confer with children, encourage them to realize that they can determine the appropriate sign without figuring out the totals. For example, in this case 8(1) can be disregarded since there are eight pennies on each board, and 2(10) + 1(5) can be exchanged for 1(25) to determine that the amounts on the boards are equivalent. Play ends when eight statements have been made. At that point players can determine what they have in their "piggy banks"—that is, the total on their boards at the end of the game.

Supporting the Investigation

☀ As children play the game, encourage them to look for equivalence, rather than using arithmetic.

As children play the game, move around the room and confer with a few groups. Encourage them to look for equivalence, rather than using arithmetic and determining totals.

Inside One Classroom

Conferring with Children at Work

Philip: I have 41 cents. *(The board has one penny, one nickel, one dime, and one quarter.)*

Trish (the teacher): How do you know?

Philip: I added it up. A quarter is 25 plus 10…35…plus 5…40. So it's 41.

Trish: What about you, Isaac? *(On his board he has three pennies, one nickel, one dime, and one quarter.)*

Isaac: I think maybe 47. *(Guessing.)*

Trish: Do you have more or less than Philip? Let's look at the board. Is there another way to tell without adding it all up?

Isaac: He has more, I know. Wait…maybe I do. Because we both have this. *(Puts his hand on top of the nickels, dimes, and quarters.)* But I have 3 pennies!

Trish: So who has more?

Isaac: I do!

Trish: So let's make the sign point to Philip's.

Continued on next page

Author's Notes

Trish questions to understand the child's thinking—how he determined 41. He easily adds fives and tens.

Encouraging Isaac to examine the expression without doing arithmetic challenges him to stop guessing—to consider equivalent expressions.

TRADES, JUMPS, AND STOPS

Continued from previous page

Isaac: I guess I have 43 cents, because I have 2 more pennies!

Appendix E   **Student recording sheet for Piggy Bank**

Name _____   Date _____

Name Philip   Name Isaac

1 ⑤	=	1 ⑤
1 ⑤ + ㉕	>	1 ⑤ + ⑩
1 ⑤ + ⑩ + ⑩	<	② + ⑩ + ①⑳
①① + ⑤ + ⑩ + ⑩	<	㉚ + ⑤ + ⑩ + ⑤②

© 2007 Catherine Twomey Fosnot from *Contexts for Learning Mathematics* (Portsmouth, NH: Heinemann). This page may be reproduced for classroom use only.

TRADES, JUMPS, AND STOPS   87

Figure 1

Assessment Tips

Notice the strategies children are using as they play the game. Can they add tens and fives easily? Do they determine the coins to take by easily exchanging, for example, a dime for two nickels? As they discuss which symbol to record, are they adding up all the amounts tediously, or are they looking for equivalence and eliminating expressions that are identical?

Reflections on the Day

Today's minilesson encouraged children to explore equivalent combinations of coins, each of which equaled 50 cents. By asking questions to determine the denominations of the hidden coins, they had opportunities to consider equivalent possibilities. As they played Piggy Bank, they were supported in examining statements without resorting to arithmetic. Here emphasis was placed on strategies such as comparison, substitution, and elimination (or "canceling") to determine whether the appropriate relational symbol to place between two quantities would be $<$, $>$, or $=$.

The Piggy Bank

Materials Needed

Coins for the minilesson (one quarter, three dimes, and five nickels)

Bag of coins (quarters, nickels, dimes, and pennies)—one bag per pair of children

Piggy Bank game cards from Day Two—one deck per pair of children

Piggy Bank game board from Day Two— one per child

Student recording sheet for Piggy Bank (Appendix E)— one per pair of children

Drawing paper— one sheet per pair of children

Large chart pad and easel

Markers

As on Day Two, the day begins with a minilesson—"twenty questions" to determine the coins hidden in your hand. The total amount is again 50 cents, but the coins are different. The children play Piggy Bank again, and then a math congress is convened for a whole-class discussion on strategies. Two-column proofs are introduced as a representation of children's reasoning.

Day Three Outline

Minilesson: "Twenty Questions" for Fifty Cents

☀ Ask children to share the thinking underlying their questions as they try to determine the value of the coins hidden in your hand.

☀ Record the solutions in equation form and ask children to discuss the possible exchanges made as you went from Problem #1 to Problem #2.

Developing the Context

☀ Remind children how to play Piggy Bank.

Supporting the Investigation

☀ Challenge children to exchange coins to compare expressions.

Preparing for the Math Congress

☀ Ask children to choose one of the strategies they used to compare expressions and record it on drawing paper.

Facilitating the Math Congress

☀ Represent children's strategies in a two-column proof.

☀ Have the children discuss each strategy and ask any questions they may have.

Minilesson: "Twenty Questions" for Fifty Cents

(10–15 minutes)

This mental math minilesson uses the format of "twenty questions" to provide children with opportunities to think about equivalence. There are two problems; each uses coins totaling 50 cents. As on Day Two, place the coins in your closed palm without allowing children to identify them. Announce the total value of the coins (50 cents) in your hand. Record the questions and answers on chart paper or the chalkboard as you proceed, keeping track of the number of questions it takes for the class to determine the exact combinations of coins. Have children share the thinking underlying their questions.

> **Problem #1:** 3 dimes, 4 nickels (50 cents)
> **Problem #2:** 1 quarter, 5 nickels (50 cents)

After the children solve the two problems, write them in an equation form. When the equation is written at the end, children will need to examine what

$$\text{Equation: } 3 \, (\!10\!) + 4 (\!5\!) = 1 \, (\!25\!) + 5 (\!5\!)$$

you might have exchanged as you went from Problem #1 to Problem #2. Encourage them to examine the equation by decomposing and exchanging rather than adding to find the totals.

- ☀ Ask children to share the thinking underlying their questions as they try to determine the value of the coins hidden in your hand.

- ☀ Record the solutions in equation form and ask children to discuss the possible exchanges made as you went from Problem #1 to Problem #2.

Behind the Numbers

The coins have been carefully chosen to encourage children to consider substitution and equivalence. Problem #1 has no quarters. Children will most likely question about quarters first. Once quarters and pennies are ruled out, children only need to consider the combinations of dimes and nickels that are possible. Problem #2 has one quarter; once this is established, children only need to consider ways to make 25 cents. This logic, however, may still be out of reach for many children. You should therefore question them on the logic underlying their questioning. The limited number of possible questions (twenty) is an important constraint in this activity as it pushes children to consider what makes a good question.

A Portion of the Minilesson

Inside One Classroom

Author's Notes

The context of coins helps children realize what they are doing as they seek to establish equivalence.

Trish (the teacher): So you have figured out what I have, both times…and you did it with fewer than twenty questions. Wow! Nice job. You are getting good at this! So let me write an equation for the two problems. *(Writes:)*

$$3(10) + 4(5) = 1(25) + 5(5)$$

Is this a true statement?

Juanita: Yes, because 30, that's 3 dimes…and 20 cents more is 50. On the other side is 25 and 25. That's 50, too. So 50 equals 50. You had 50 cents both times.

Trish: So one way is to do all the arithmetic. That convinces us, doesn't it? I wonder…are there other ways we could know, too…without doing all the arithmetic? Maria?

Trish challenges the children to consider the expressions as objects.

Maria: I know a dime is 2 nickels…and a quarter is 2 dimes and a nickel.

(Trish writes:)

$$3(10) + 4(5) = 1(25) + 5(5)$$
$$1(10) = 2(5)$$
$$1(25) = 2(10) + 1(5)$$

Trish writes the givens—the true statements underlying Maria's argument. By encouraging the whole community to consider what Maria's next steps might be, Trish enables others to develop similar arguments.

Trish: Let's look at what Maria said so far. Don't tell us yet how that helped you, Maria. Let's see if we can figure out what you did next. Turn to the person next to you and talk about Maria's thinking so far, and then discuss what you think she will say next. *(After some pair talk, the whole-class conversation resumes.)* Carlos? What did you and Katie talk about?

Pair talk provides reflection time and implicitly says that we are a community engaged in thinking. We consider each other's ideas.

Carlos: She made it the same. We agree, a dime is 2 nickels, and a quarter is 2 dimes and a nickel. So she can trade and rearrange some more.

Trish: Is that how you knew, Maria?

Maria: Yep. Both sides have a quarter and 5 nickels.

*(Trish writes Maria's actions to the right.
To the left she writes the resulting equations:)*

$1(25) + 5(5) = 2(10) + 1(5) + 5(5)$	Trade
$1(25) + 5(5) = 2(10) + 2(5) + 4(5)$	Rearrange
$1(25) + 5(5) = 3(10) + 4(5)$	Trade

By writing down Maria's actions on the right, Trish introduces two-column proofs. This modeling also leaves a visible representation of Maria's thinking for others to read and reflect on. Reading others' mathematics, following their arguments, and determining if the argument holds is an important part of what mathematicians do.

Developing the Context

The purpose of playing Piggy Bank again is to provide more experience with determining which relational symbol (<, >, =) is appropriate to compare two expressions, and specifically to continue encouraging children to check for equivalency without doing all the arithmetic to determine the totals.

As on Day Two, children play the game in pairs and take turns picking a card from the Piggy Bank deck, choosing coins to place on their boards, and recording equations. The card determines the amount they can place on their board. Remind children that the greater-than or less-than sign always points to the smaller amount.

☀ Remind children how to play Piggy Bank.

Supporting the Investigation

As you walk around today supporting and conferring with children as they play the game, challenge them to exchange coins as a way of determining which relational sign (<, >, =) to use, rather than resorting to doing all the arithmetic. This is harder for children than you might think. They often need to do the arithmetic just to be sure. Allow them to do so, but then suggest that they try to defend their thinking in another way as well. Support them in using an exchange of coins to compare the expressions.

☀ Challenge children to exchange coins to compare expressions.

Preparing for the Math Congress

The upcoming math congress will focus on strategies such as decomposing amounts and making exchanges. You will represent a few of the children's strategies in a two-column proof (as in Inside One Classroom on pages 28 and 29). Before you convene the congress, ask the children to select one of the statements from their Piggy Bank recording sheets and to think about one strategy they used to determine which sign to use. Distribute drawing paper and ask children to write down their strategies.

Do not expect children to record their strategies using a two-column proof. Let them just write about what they did using pictures of coins and words. On the other hand, if you see any children trying to use the two-column format, help them to do so.

☀ Ask children to choose one of the strategies they used to compare expressions and record it on drawing paper.

Facilitating the Math Congress

In this congress, have several children share one of their statements from their recording sheets as well as the strategy they used to determine which relational sign to use. As they share, record (on chart paper or the chalkboard) a two-column representation of the strategy. After each child shares, ask the community to consider the strategy and to discuss areas of agreement or any questions they may have.

☀ Represent children's strategies in a two-column proof.

☀ Have the children discuss each strategy and ask any questions they may have.

A Portion of the Math Congress

Trish (the teacher): Isaac and Olivia, tell us about the one you chose to share.

Olivia: I had 3 nickels and 2 quarters and 2 pennies. Isaac had 2 nickels, 3 dimes, 1 quarter, and 2 pennies. We decided it was equal.

(Trish writes:)

$$3(5) + 2(25) + 2(1) = 2(5) + 3(10) + 1(25) + 2(1)$$

Trish: And tell us how you decided this was true.

Olivia: We knew 2 dimes and a nickel made a quarter. So Isaac traded.

(Trish writes:)

$$3(5) + 2(25) + 2(1) \; ? \; 2(5) + 3(10) + 1(25) + 2(1)$$
$$2(10) + 1(5) = 1(25) \qquad \text{Trade}$$
$$3(5) + 2(25) + 2(1) \; ? \; 1(5) + 1(10) + 2(25) + 2(1)$$

Isaac: And we both had 2 pennies and 2 quarters so we knew that part was the same and so they didn't matter.

Trish: Wow. You said a lot there. Let's see what everyone thinks. Isaac said that the 2 pennies and the 2 quarters don't matter because they are on both sides. Turn to the person next to you and talk about this. Is he right?

Heather: He's right. They are the same.

Trish: So can I erase them?

Heather: I don't think you can erase them.

Isaac: Cross 'em out. You could do that. Because we both have them. They don't matter. And a dime is 2 nickels. So, see, they are equal. So we put an equal sign.

Author's Notes

Trish records for the community but she challenges children to justify the moves they make. She pushes them to provide a convincing argument.

The actions are recorded on the right.

Children are supported in developing their own rules as long as the community agrees with the logic. The rules that mathematicians use in their proofs were constructed in a similar fashion over the history of the evolution of mathematics, proven and/or accepted in a mathematical community, and then used to prove more elaborate ideas.

Continued on next page

Continued from previous page

Trish: Does everybody agree that if the same thing is on both sides we can cross them out?

(Everyone accepts this so Trish writes):

$3⑤ + 2㉕ + 2① \ ?\ 2⑤ + 3⑩ + 1㉕ + 2①$

$\qquad\qquad\qquad 1⑤ + 2⑩ = 1㉕$ Trade

$3⑤ + 2㉕ + 2① \ ?\ 1⑤ + 1⑩ + 2㉕ + 2①$

$3⑤ + \cancel{2㉕} + \cancel{2①} \ ?\ 1⑤ + 1⑩ + \cancel{2㉕} + \cancel{2①}$ Isaac's cross-out rule

$\qquad\qquad 1⑩ = 2⑤$ Trade

$\qquad\qquad 3⑤ = 3⑤$

$3⑤ + 2㉕ + 2① = 3⑤ + 2㉕ + 2①$

Here Trish works to establish a "cancellation" law and to establish equivalence. Although mathematicians will eliminate extraneous equivalent expressions, this is difficult for children to understand. They often are willing to cross numbers out or to say that equivalent amounts don't matter, but they want to hold the amount "in storage" rather than eliminate it.

The rule is owned by Isaac and thus is named for him. Since he said "cross out," it is called the "cross-out rule." Emphasis is placed on invention and the logic of arguments in this community of young mathematicians at work.

Reflections on the Day

Today children continued to explore equivalent combinations of coins equaling 50 cents. By asking questions to determine the denominations of the hidden coins, they considered equivalent values. Playing Piggy Bank again provided additional opportunities to examine the value of expressions without resorting to arithmetic. Emphasis was placed on strategies such as comparison, substitution, and crossing out ("cancellation") to determine whether the appropriate relational symbol to compare two expressions or values would be <, >, or =. Children were introduced to two-column proofs and encouraged to examine mathematical arguments.

DAY FOUR

Foreign Coins and Trading for Dimes

Materials Needed

Two bags of coins for the minilesson (one bag containing one quarter, three dimes, four nickels, and one foreign coin *(c)* (from Appendix F); the second bag containing one quarter, two dimes, six nickels, and one foreign coin *(c)*

Trading for Dimes game cards (Appendix G)—one deck per pair of children

Student recording sheet for Trading for Dimes (Appendix H)—one per pair of children, with extras available

Dime wrappers— several per pair of children

Large chart pad and easel

Markers

The day begins again with a minilesson—"twenty questions" to determine the value of coins hidden in two bags. Today there is a twist, however. A foreign coin is introduced as a variable; the value of the coin is unknown. The class then plays the Trading for Dimes game with integer cards, which encourage children to trade equivalent amounts. Emphasis is placed on tens to support the use of landmark numbers in establishing equivalence.

Day Four Outline

Minilesson: "Twenty Questions"

* Ask children to share the thinking underlying their questions as they try to determine the value of the coins hidden in two bags and whether or not those values are equivalent.

* Ask children to determine the appropriate relational sign to compare the values.

* Explain that each bag includes a foreign coin after children have determined the value of all the other coins.

Developing the Context

* Model how to play Trading for Dimes.

Supporting the Investigation

* As children play the game, encourage them to make tens and look for equivalence.

Minilesson: "Twenty Questions" (10–15 minutes)

This mental math minilesson uses the format of "twenty questions" again to provide children with opportunities to think about equivalence. Use two bags today (instead of your hand); do not tell children the total value of the coins in each. Children work to establish whether the total value of coins in each bag is the same. Record coins as children determine them, using the appropriate relational sign (<, >, =) in the statement (as shown in Inside One Classroom, page 32). Have children share their thinking as they determine which sign is appropriate.

Problem #1: Bag #1: 1 quarter, 3 dimes, 4 nickels, 1 foreign coin (c)

Bag #2: 1 quarter, 2 dimes, 6 nickels, 1 foreign coin (c)

Problem #2: Bag #1: 1 quarter, 2 dimes, 4 nickels, 1 foreign coin (c)

Bag #2: 1 quarter, 2 dimes, 6 nickels, 1 foreign coin (c)

As you proceed, record what the community knows for certain and ask children to determine the appropriate relational sign to compare the values. As each new determination is made, discuss whether or not to change the sign and how they know. Announce that you have a foreign coin in each bag after they have determined all the other coins and think they are done. Explain that although you don't know what the foreign coins are worth, you are certain that they are identical.

☀ Ask children to share the thinking underlying their questions as they try to determine the value of the coins hidden in two bags and whether or not those values are equivalent.

☀ Ask children to determine the appropriate relational sign to compare the values.

☀ Explain that each bag includes a foreign coin after children have determined the value of all the other coins.

Behind the Numbers

The foreign coin has been added to engage children in determining equivalence of expressions with a variable added. The value in U.S. money of the coin is unknown. For Problem #1, the value of the coins in Bag #1 equals that in Bag #2 without the foreign coin. Each bag contains the same foreign coin, c, so the bags contain equal values no matter what the foreign coin is worth.

Problem #2 is structured to involve children in considering unequal amounts. Here, as long as the foreign coin in each bag is identical, the total values of coins contained in each remain unequal. Expect children to have a spirited discussion about the addition of the foreign coin. Some will say it is not possible to decide if the bag values are equivalent without knowing what the value of the foreign coin is. Children who are still adding amounts up, doing all the arithmetic to determine which relational sign to use, will be especially resistant to accepting the idea that a determination can be made.

Inside One Classroom

Author's Notes

Trish (the teacher): So far you have figured out that there is 1 quarter in each bag and 2 dimes in this bag on the left. Let me write that down. What sign should I use so far?

Several voices: Greater than.

Trish: Why? Sam?

Trish challenges the children to consider the expressions as objects. Which is more, or are they equivalent?

Sam: Well, the quarters are the same, but the bag on the left has 2 dimes.

(Trish writes:)

$$1\,\text{㉕} + 2\,\text{⑩} > 1\,\text{㉕}$$

Trish: OK. Do you have more questions for me?

Juanita: Are there more than 2 dimes in the other bag?

Trish: Yes.

Kelly: Are there 3?

Trish: Exactly? *(Child nods.)* Yes. So let's write this down. Now you know the quarters and the dimes. Which sign do we need?

Juanita: You have to turn the sign around. Make it point to 1 quarter and 2 dimes.

(Trish writes:)

$$1\,\text{㉕} + 2\,\text{⑩} < 1\,\text{㉕} + 3\,\text{⑩}$$

(Discussion continues until the following equation is determined and pennies are ruled out:)

$$1\,\text{㉕} + 2\,\text{⑩} + 6\,\text{⑤} = 1\,\text{㉕} + 3\,\text{⑩} + 4\,\text{⑤}$$

Trish: You think we are done now, don't you? Actually there is one more coin in each bag and it is the same type of coin in each bag.

The variable is introduced.

Juanita: What is it?

Continued on next page

Continued from previous page

Trish: I don't know what this type of coin is worth. They are foreign coins that I got a long time ago when I was traveling. I put one in each bag. Let's call it *c* for coin because we don't know what it's worth. Here's what we know so far. *(Writes:)*

$$1\,\textcircled{25} + 2\,\textcircled{10} + 6\,\textcircled{5} + c \ ? \ 1\,\textcircled{25} + 3\,\textcircled{10} + 4\,\textcircled{5} + c$$

What sign should we use?

Sam: We can't do it if you don't tell us. How can we add it if we don't know what it is?

Trish: Do you have to add it?

Rosie: If it's a nickel, it's still equal.

Juanita: It works for a penny or a dime, too.

Trish: Does it work for other numbers, too?

Keshawn: It works for any number, because it's the same in both bags.

Isaac: You don't have to know what it is. If it's the same coin and it's in both bags, you don't have to worry about it. It's the same on both sides so it's still the equal sign.

Trish: Could *c* be any amount? Are Keshawn and Isaac right? Would this be true no matter what *c* is? *(Writes in equal sign:)*

$$1\,\textcircled{25} + 2\,\textcircled{10} + 6\,\textcircled{5} + c = 1\,\textcircled{25} + 3\,\textcircled{10} + 4\,\textcircled{5} + c$$

Isaac: Yep. Because of my cross-out rule.

Trish: Doesn't it matter what *c* is?

Michael: No, *c* could be any number. As long as you give both bags the same, it doesn't matter what the value of the *c* coin is.

If children are still using arithmetic, this problem seems impossible to work with. One of the biggest stumbling blocks for older students when they encounter algebra is that they do not have a strong sense of equivalence.

Trish encourages children to consider several numbers as a way of developing the idea of a variable.

Trish challenges the children to generalize. When they have constructed their own rules in the community, they use them to justify and prove.

Assessment Tips

Notice today the children's responses to the introduction of the foreign coins. Which children were confident that arithmetic was unnecessary? Which could generalize about *c* being any number? Which understood that the addition of *c* to each expression of a bag's value didn't change the relationship of equality or inequality? Which children used substitution strategies? Which employed the use of "crossing out"?

Use the landscape of learning graphic on page 12 as a way to record individual pathways representative of children's growth and development.

You might find it helpful to make copies of the graphic, one for each child, and record growth and pathways by shading in the landmarks as children pass them.

Developing the Context

☀ Model how to play Trading for Dimes.

Explain to children that today they will play a new game called Trading for Dimes. Have the children sit in a circle. Play the game with one child in the center of the circle as a way to introduce the game and model how it is played. Boards and coins are not used in this game.

▦ Object of the Game

The objective of Trading for Dimes is to get enough dimes to trade for a coin wrapper—which, when filled, is worth five dollars. Play is cooperative and exchanges are recorded as equations. Coins are not used in this version; this will act as a constraint to hinder arithmetic strategies and to encourage children to trade instead.

▦ Directions for Playing Trading for Dimes

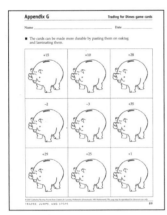

Children play the game in pairs. Each pair of children has a deck of Trading for Dimes game cards (Appendix G) and a recording sheet (Appendix H). Have extra recording sheets available because pairs will probably need more than one.

Children take turns laying out four Trading for Dimes game cards. The cards determine the amount of money children can place in their piggy banks, but this time, instead of taking coins, they write down the amounts on the recording sheet and then write down the possible combinations of coins they can trade for. For example, if two players (working as partners) select +8, +14, +15, −5, they can trade for three dimes and two pennies because this amount would be equivalent in total value. On the recording sheet, children write:

$$+8 + 14 + 15 - 5 = + 10 + 10 + 10 + 2$$

Explain that the plus and minus signs symbolize whether they are getting money for their piggy bank or losing it.

Play continues with four more cards laid out and a second equation written. At any point when the extras left over after all trades for dimes are completed (such as the + 2 in the above example) can be combined with extras left over from other rounds, they can be written as an equation as well. All trades must be recorded as equations.

The objective is to accrue 50 dimes in order to get a coin wrapper. The children take the recording sheet to the banker (you or a child designated for this role), who checks to be sure that the players requesting a wrapper have 50 dimes, before giving them the wrapper.

Supporting the Investigation

As children play the game, move around the room and confer with a few groups. Encourage them to make tens and to look for equivalence, rather than using arithmetic and adding up totals.

☀ As children play the game, encourage them to make tens and look for equivalence.

Reflections on the Day

Today children continued to write statements using the relational signs <, >, and =, and they were introduced to variables with the context of the foreign coins. At this point your students are probably beginning to develop several strategies to establish equivalence, (such as comparison, substitution, and "crossing out"). As they played Trading for Dimes, they were encouraged to make tens. As the unit continues, tens will continue to be used to encourage children to treat expressions as objects, rather than using arithmetic to calculate totals.

Using the Double Number Line

Materials Needed

A string of 100 connecting cubes hung on a chalkboard or whiteboard. The string should include two different colors of cubes arranged in alternating groups of five cubes of each color.

The Masloppy Family Goes to New York City (Appendix A)

Student recording sheet for the subtract five investigation (Appendix I)—
one per pair of children

Large chart paper—
one sheet per pair of children

Large chart pad and easel

Markers

The day begins again with a minilesson, but this time it is a string of statements and children need to establish whether the equal or not equal sign should be used to make them true. Emphasis is placed on ten and five as landmark numbers to be used in establishing equivalence with the use of a string of connecting cubes (or a whiteboard number line). A new investigation is then introduced; it focuses on substituting equivalent expressions as a shortcut way to subtract. Children then make posters in preparation for a math congress, to be held on Day Six.

Day Five Outline

Minilesson: True or Not True?

☀ Work on a string of problems designed to support children in making equivalent expressions.

☀ Use the string of connecting cubes as a double number line to represent children's strategies.

Developing the Context

☀ Introduce the strategy of subtracting five by adding five and subtracting ten.

☀ Ask children to investigate whether this strategy works and, if so, why.

Supporting the Investigation

☀ Encourage children to try out the strategy with several problems.

☀ Suggest that they represent their thinking on a double number line.

Preparing for the Math Congress

☀ Ask children to make posters explaining why they think the strategy works.

Minilesson: True or Not True? (10–15 minutes)

This mental math minilesson uses the format of a string of several statements. Children need to decide if the statements are true or not true. As children share their thinking, represent one side of the statement on the top of the string of connecting cubes and the other on the bottom. Group the numbers exactly to match the child's strategy. For example, in analyzing $5 + 4 + 10 = 10 + 5 + 5$, some children may just compare the $5 + 5$ to $5 + 4$. This can be represented in several ways, depending on what the child says. If a child says, "I knew the tens were the same, and 5 plus 4 is 1 less than 5 plus 5," you can draw the following: Implicit in this strategy is the commutative property of addition. Encourage the children to discuss whether or not the order in which the numbers are added matters. As you progress through the string, encourage children to

☀ Work on a string of problems designed to support children in making equivalent expressions.

☀ Use the string of connecting cubes as a double number line to represent children's strategies.

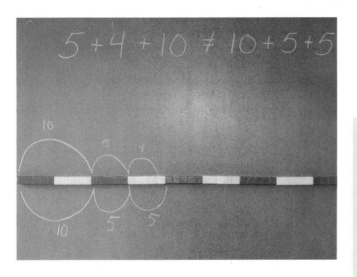

look for efficient ways of deciding whether the statement is true. Represent their strategies on the double number line to allow the community to look for equivalence, and then change the sign appropriately (keeping = or making it ≠).

String of problems:

$$5 + 4 + 10 = 10 + 5 + 5$$

$$13 + 4 + 7 - 4 = 3 + 13 + 4$$

$$13 + 9 + 6 = 5 + 10 + 13$$

$$6 + 3 + 10 = 8 + 3 + 7 + 2$$

Behind the Numbers

The numbers in the string have been chosen carefully to support children in making equivalent expressions to determine whether the statements are true. The numbers in the first problem are almost the same on both sides. The only difference is the 4 on the left as compared with the 5 on the right. No arithmetic should be necessary to determine that the first statement is not true (the sign should be ≠), but several strategies may be used, and you may find that some children still need to do the arithmetic to evaluate the truth of the statement. The commutative property will probably come up because of the placement of the tens. The second problem introduces the idea of 4 − 4, thus encouraging children to simplify the expressions by using the commutative and associative properties. The third problem has two thirteens, which can be "canceled," but more thought will be needed for dealing with $9 + 6 = 5 + 10$. You will probably hear comments such as, "You just gain one and lose one, so the total stays the same" (compensation). This is an important idea in the development of an understanding of equivalence. The last problem may encourage children to use the associative property if they know combinations of numbers that add up to ten. The statement is not true; the sign should be ≠.

A Portion of the Minilesson

Author's Notes

Trish (the teacher): Let's try to make it as simple as we can, as mathematicians do. Let's look for nice, efficient ways without a lot of work for this one. *(Writes:)*

$$13 + 4 + 7 - 4 = 3 + 13 + 4$$

Efficiency and elegance of solution are valued in this community. Trish challenges the children to consider the expressions as objects.

Mia Chiara: Well, I knew 13 plus 7 is 20. Then I saw 4 and minus 4, so that side is 20. It has a 4 and if you take it away… Then the other side is 13 plus 7 because 3 plus 4 is 7.

(Trish draws jumps of 13 + 7 on top and 13 + 3 + 4 on the bottom.)

Trish draws the jumps on the top and bottom of the string of cubes to provide a representation for a discussion of equivalence.

Aidan: They both have 13 and on one side there's a 7 and on the other side there's a 3 plus 4.

Juanita: Three plus 4 equals 7, so they both have the same on both sides.

Delia: You don't have to bother with 4 minus 4, because you're taking away what you just added.

"Doing" and "undoing" with integers is important to algebraic thinking. The number line is used to examine the jumps.

Alec: I wouldn't bother looking at the 13 or the 4, because they are on both sides. And 7 take away 4 is 3, so 3 equals 3.

Trish: What would 4 minus 4 look like on this number line?

Delia: It would look like 4 and 4 back, or chalk dust because it's nothing.

(Trish adds a jump of 4 to the previously drawn jumps and then goes back 4.)

Chynna: You don't even need to do that. It's 13 and 13, so cross them out. Cross out the two 4s, so it's just 7 minus 4 equals 3.

Some of the children are beginning to eliminate and simplify the equation.

Developing the Context

☀ Introduce the strategy of subtracting five by adding five and subtracting ten.

☀ Ask children to investigate whether this strategy works and, if so, why.

Remind the children about the story of the Masloppy family. Tell them that you once knew a boy just like Nicholas. He loved to organize things, too. One day he told you that he knew a fast way to subtract five. He said that instead of taking five away he added five and then took ten away. Encourage the children to try this on a few problems—for example, 32 − 5 = ? Solve it as 32 + 5 − 10. Do not write 32 − 5 = 32 + 5 − 10. At this point, the children have explored so many equations that the representation may make the inquiry too easy. Instead, pass out recording sheets (Appendix I), and have the children work in pairs to figure out if the strategy works and why.

Supporting the Investigation

As you walk around supporting and conferring with children, have them try out the strategy with several problems to make sure that the strategy is clear. Many children will be surprised and amazed that it works each time. Enjoy their surprise and wonder with them why the strategy works. Encourage them to figure out why. The double number line (or the string of cubes), can be a helpful model for understanding; encourage children to represent the steps on it. If they figure out why the strategy works—because $+5 - 10 = -5$— you can challenge them to find similar strategies for subtracting six or seven. Challenge them to generalize this for any number to be subtracted.

☀ Encourage children to try out the strategy with several problems.

☀ Suggest that they represent their thinking on a double number line.

Preparing for the Math Congress

The congress you will be holding on Day Six will focus on equivalence, specifically that -5 can be exchanged for $+5 - 10$. To prepare for the congress, ask the children to make posters of their proofs, of why they think the strategy works. Explain that mathematicians write up their ideas so that they may convince others; they don't just make a list of the mathematical steps they used.

☀ Ask children to make posters explaining why they think the strategy works.

Reflections on the Day

Today in the minilesson children analyzed the truth of mathematical statements and were once again encouraged to treat expressions as objects and to use strategies such as substitution and "canceling," rather than arithmetic. They also examined the commutative and associative properties. In the investigation children explored how substitution can be helpful for operations with whole numbers, as well.

Using the Double Number Line

Materials Needed

String of connecting cubes from Day Five (or whiteboard number line)

Students' completed recording sheets (Appendix I) and posters from Day Five

Sticky notes— one pad per child

Large chart pad and easel

Markers

The day begins again with a minilesson, a string of mathematical statements to be analyzed in a way similar to that used on Day Five. Emphasis is placed on using the associative and commutative properties for addition to make equivalent expressions, and the use of "canceling" and substitution strategies is supported. A "gallery walk" is then held to prepare for today's math congress on the work of Day Five. The congress focuses on how equivalent expressions can be substituted in an equation to make subtraction easier. The conversation in the congress is also about the importance of generalization and on what makes a good proof.

Day Six Outline

Minilesson: True or Not True?

☀ Work on a string of problems designed to support children in making equivalent expressions.

☀ Use the string of connecting cubes as a double number line to represent children's strategies.

Preparing for the Math Congress (continued from Day Five)

☀ Conduct a gallery walk to give children a chance to look at each other's posters from Day Five.

☀ Plan for a math congress discussion about why the strategy works. Think about scaffolding the discussion toward generalizing about equivalence and substitution and establishing what makes a good mathematical justification.

Facilitating the Math Congress

☀ After discussing why the strategy works, encourage the children to think about whether the strategy would work with other numbers.

Minilesson: True or Not True? (10–15 minutes)

This mental math minilesson uses the format of a string of several related statements. Children need to decide if the statements are true or not true. In this string the statements are all true, so the equal sign does not need to be changed. As children share their thinking, represent one side of the equation on the top of the string of connecting cubes and the other side on the bottom. Group the numbers exactly to match each child's strategy. The numbers have been chosen carefully to support children in making equivalent expressions as a strategy that can be used to determine whether the statements are true. The problems have been crafted to encourage a conversation on the commutative and associative properties for addition.

☀ Work on a string of problems designed to support children in making equivalent expressions.

☀ Use the string of connecting cubes as a double number line to represent children's strategies.

String of related problems:

$$25 + 4 = 4 + 10 + 10 + 5$$

$$25 + 6 + 4 - 6 = 4 + 10 + 10 + 5$$

$$10 + 10 + 5 + 13 = 13 + 28 + 25 - 28$$

$$10 + 15 + 13 = 18 + 10 + 10$$

Preparing for the Math Congress
(continued from Day Five)

Before you start the math congress, stage a gallery walk to look at the posters. Give children a few minutes to revisit their work from Day Five and make any last-minute changes on their posters. Then display the posters around the room. Pass out small pads of sticky notes so children can record comments or questions as they walk around. These notes can be placed directly onto the posters. Give children fifteen minutes to read and comment on the mathematics on the posters. Then give everyone a few minutes to read the sticky notes on their own posters before you start the math congress.

Behind the Numbers

The first equation in the string uses the landmark numbers of 10, 5, and 25 to encourage children to group (10, 10, and 5 into 25). The double number line can be used to explore why it is OK to do this (because of the associative property). In the next step, children are faced with proving that $25 + 4 = 4 + 25$, which is possible because of the commutative property. The representation on the double number line supports children in generalizing these properties.

The second problem adds the expression $6 - 6$ to one expression in order to suggest the importance of grouping. Help children realize that although these numbers are not next to each other in the problem, when re-arranged they "cancel" each other out and now the equation is identical to the first. The third problem repeats the same idea, but employs greater numbers ($28 - 28$) to make the arithmetic more challenging. If some children are still proceeding to perform operations from left to right with tedious arithmetic, these numbers serve to discourage that strategy. The last problem is a little more difficult because it requires children to decompose numbers in order to make their own equivalent expressions.

▨ Tips for Structuring the Math Congress

You will probably see several ways that children have explored the strategy of subtracting five by adding five and then subtracting ten:

❖ Some children may have used the strategy to solve several problems and then just assumed that it will always work. Here the view of "proof" is: just try the strategy many times.

❖ Other children may have drawn a representation on a double number line to show that $+ 5 - 10$ lands in the same place as -5. In this view of "proof," it is sufficient to show a visual representation of the answer.

☀ Conduct a gallery walk to give children a chance to look at each other's posters from Day Five.

☀ Plan for a math congress discussion about why the strategy works. Think about scaffolding the discussion toward generalizing about equivalence and substitution and establishing what makes a good mathematical justification.

❖ Other children, also using a double number line to show that + 5 − 10 lands in the same place as −5, may use the representation to explain equivalence and to generalize about the part-whole relations—that the number being subtracted (5) and the number being added (5) must equal 10. Sometimes one example is sufficient, if it allows the relationships to be understood and generalized. The open double number line representation may produce a powerful moment in which you can challenge your students to use the example to generalize.

❖ Still others may have written equations, such as $32 − 5 = 32 + 5 − 10$. These children may be able to explain that $+ 5 − 10 = −5$ and to generalize for other cases, such as $−6 = + 4 − 10$ and $−7 = + 3 − 10$, etc.

Plan on scaffolding the congress toward a discussion of why the strategy works and toward generalizing about equivalence and the part-whole relations ($5 + 5 = 10$; $6 + 4 = 10$; $a + b = c$). You will also want to scaffold toward a conversation on proof—on what makes a good justification. By starting with children who have merely tried the strategy in several cases, you can challenge the community to consider whether doing so is enough justification for concluding that it will always work. Move next to examining either equations or number line representations of the strategy. Here you can guide the conversation to a generalization about equivalence and substitution, with an eye toward establishing what makes a good mathematical justification.

Facilitating the Math Congress

☀ After discussing why the strategy works, encourage the children to think about whether the strategy would work with other numbers.

After the gallery walk, convene the community in the meeting area for a math congress. Have two or three pairs of children present their posters. Facilitate a conversation around the important mathematical ideas and the justifications for why it works to add five and subtract ten in order to subtract five. Guide the conversation toward other examples, such as subtracting six or seven, instead of five. If you began by subtracting ten, what would you add?

Inside One Classroom

A Portion of the Math Congress

Author's Notes

Trish (the teacher): So Colleen and Juanita, you showed us several examples...and then you said, "So we know it always works." Have they convinced us that the strategy will always work? Is just trying it out several times enough for us to be certain that it will always work? Maybe in the next problem you try, it won't work. We might not want to use it if we can't be certain.

Olivia: I don't think trying it out lots of times is enough. I think we have to know why it works. And that's what's bothering me. I don't know why it works!

Continued on next page

The community is guided to consider what is necessary to make a convincing argument—what is sufficient to support a generalization? Trish's question goes right to the heart of algebraic thinking.

Continued from previous page

Trish: Hmm…knowing why might help us be sure it will always work. What is going on here? Rosie, you and Jasmine have an interesting way for us to look at this. Show us what you did.

Rosie: We made a number line.

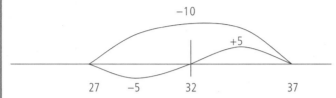

The double number line represents the equivalence.

We did the boy's strategy on top, and we did 32 minus 5 on the bottom. We got 27 both times.

Trish: Let me write down an equation for what you said so we can all think about this. On the top is 32 plus 5 minus 10, and on the bottom is 32 minus 5. *(Writes:)*

$$32 + 5 - 10 = 32 - 5$$

Trish writes the equation next to the number line representation.

Kelly: We could cross out the 32s. I think we could also add 5 first and then subtract 10.

Kelly makes use of the cross-out strategy and the commutative property as she explores a justification.

Jasmine: We think it works because 5 and 5 make 10.

Trish: Who thinks you understand what Jasmine means? Who can put Jasmine and Rosie's idea in your own words? *(Several hands go up.)*

Ian: I think you mean that it works because the 5 and 5 make 10, but if we did 5 and 6 it wouldn't work.

Rosie: Yeah. See? *(Draws another number line.)* The 6 is too big. It has to be 5 and 5.

Paraphrasing is helpful. To get a discussion going with everyone in the community, Trish needs to make sure that the ideas being offered are understood. If she asked, "Does everyone get what Jasmine means?" it is likely that many children would nod their heads in response. Instead, by asking for paraphrasing, she can quickly see who is able to express the idea and she can continue discussion until everyone in the community understands what is being discussed.

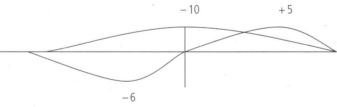

Trish: So you are saying that if we want to take away 6, we can't take away 10 and add 5. What would we add? Everybody, turn to the person next to you and talk about this. *(After some pair talk.)* Keshawn, what did you and Isaac decide?

Trish challenges the children to consider other numbers. Questions like this guide children to generalize and to examine the part-whole relations.

Keshawn: We decided it would only work if we added 4.

Isaac: Or we could take away 11 and add 5 in order to subtract 6, too.

Juanita: Oh yeah…wow…because 5 and 6 make 11…
and 4 and 6 make 10. The numbers have to add up to the number you take away.

The part-whole relations and equivalence are now the focus.

Reflections on the Day

In the minilesson today, the class had rich conversations on the associative and commutative properties for addition as children continued to examine mathematical statements. The minilesson also supported children in treating expressions as objects and using strategies of substitution and elimination (or "canceling") as they worked with equivalent expressions. The gallery walk and the congress gave the children opportunities to generalize the ideas they explored on Day Five and to consider what makes a good mathematical argument.

The Double Number Line and Foreign coins

The day begins again with a minilesson, a string of mathematical statements to be analyzed in similar fashion to those used on Days Five and Six. Emphasis continues to be placed on the use of the associative and commutative properties of addition in making equivalent expressions, and the use of "cancellation" and substitution strategies is supported. Today a variable, n, is introduced, and children are encouraged to examine what happens when $n = 0$. In a subsequent investigation with foreign coins (used as unknowns), children are challenged to figure out their numerical values. The double number line continues to be used as a helpful model and strategies such as doing and undoing are discussed.

Day Seven Outline

Minilesson: True or Not True?

* Work on a string of problems designed to support children in making equivalent expressions.

* Use the string of connecting cubes or double open number line to represent children's strategies.

Developing the Context

* Introduce the foreign coins investigation and have children determine the value of coin c.

Supporting the Investigation

* Make note of children's strategies as they work to figure out the values of the other foreign coins.

Preparing for the Math Congress

* Ask children to make a list of the strategies they found most helpful in solving the foreign coins problems.

Facilitating the Math Congress

* Structure a discussion around the strategies children used and then shift the conversation to how the strategies are related.

Materials Needed

String of connecting cubes from Day Five (or at this point a drawn double number line may be sufficient)

Foreign coins (Appendix F)—one set of coins, cut out

Student recording sheet for the foreign coins investigation (Appendix J)—one per pair of children

Drawing paper— one sheet per pair of children

Large chart pad and easel

Markers

Minilesson: True or Not True? (10–15 minutes)

☀ Work on a string of problems designed to support children in making equivalent expressions.

☀ Use the string of connecting cubes or double open number line to represent children's strategies.

This mental math minilesson uses the format of a string of several related statements. Children need to decide if each statement is true or not true; if not true, they must then use the not-equal sign to make it true. As children share their thinking, represent one side of each equation on the top of the string of connecting cubes (or double open number line) and the other side on the bottom. Represent the numbers grouped to match the child's strategy. In the second problem, introduce n as a secret number that you are adding to both sides of the equation. Be sure the children understand that it is the same number on both sides. Ask them to think about what the number might be. As they generate several possibilities, try them out to help the children realize that the statement is true for any number, even for zero. In the last problem, challenge them to analyze what happens when $n = 0$.

Behind the Numbers

The numbers have been chosen carefully to support children in considering expressions as objects, using the commutative and associative properties, "canceling out," and realizing that adding the same number to each side of an equation maintains equivalence. The first two equations are identical except for the addition of n to the second. The third and fourth equations are also related. Adding 6 to each side of the fourth equation produces the third equation. Children usually see the last equation, at first, as having unequal amounts on each side of the equal sign, since n is only on one side. If they fail to consider what happens if $n = 0$, ask them to do so and help them realize that the statement is true if and only if $n = 0$.

String of related problems:

$$5 + 20 + 4 = 4 + 10 + 15$$
$$n + 5 + 20 + 4 = 4 + 10 + 15 + n$$
$$13 + 8 + 6 = 5 + 9 + 13$$
$$13 + 8 = 5 + 9 + 13 - 6$$
$$8 + 6 = 5 + 9 + n$$

A Portion of the Minilesson

Inside One Classroom

Author's Notes

Trish (the teacher): How about this next one? *(Writes:)*

$$13 + 8 = 5 + 9 + 13 - 6$$

True or not true?

Ian: True. Because 13 is on both sides so I can cancel those out. And 5 plus 9 is 14 and 14 minus 6 is 8. And 8 equals 8.

Chynna: My way is different. I started with the 9 and took 6 away. That left me with 13 plus 8 = 8 plus 13. And I know that is equal because the numbers can be turned around.

Several children share their strategies for establishing equivalence.

Continued on next page

Continued from previous page

Trish: I'll share my way, but I don't know if it will work all the time. Tell me what you think. I used the problem before this one: 13 plus 8 plus 6 equals 5 plus 9 plus 13. I took 6 away from both sides, and since I knew that problem was true I thought this one had to be, too. What do you think?

Rosie: That works! All the time...because if you add or subtract any number to both sides and it's the same number it will stay the same.

Trish: So what about this one? True or not true? I'll use *n* to mean a secret number again. *(Writes:)*

$$8 + 6 = 5 + 9 + n$$

Mia Chiara: Not equal because if you add a number on only one side it won't work.

Trish: Talk to the person next to you about what Mia Chiara said. Do you agree? *(After a few moments of pair talk.)* Roxanna, what did your partner and you decide?

Roxanna: Mostly we agree, but what if the secret number is zero? Then it's true.

Trish: So this is true only when *n* equals zero?

Trish shares her strategy. Removing six from both sides is offered as a challenge. Until now the children have only used the numbers in the equations, "canceling" or combining them. Trish introduces a new strategy—adding the same number to both sides. Adding six eliminates the negative six. Although children agreed earlier that adding n to both sides was OK, they have not thought yet to add numbers to simplify. As a member of the community, Trish offers the possibility for consideration. This is very different from telling children a strategy and asking them all to use it.

Pair talk invites children to reflect more deeply.

Developing the Context

Remind children of the work they did with coins in the first days of this unit and the foreign coin with an unknown value. Explain that they now have so many strategies that you think they might be able to figure out the value of the foreign coin and that today you have several foreign coins (cut out from Appendix F) and some clues that will help in the investigation. Use the coin marked *c*. Explain that you don't know what it is worth, but you do know a true statement about it: when you add 10 to it, you get an amount equal to 5 + 5 + 25. Write the following as you are explaining:

$$c + 10 = 5 + 5 + 25$$

Ask the children if they have any ideas of what to do with the clue. It is likely that several children will think of 5 + 5 as 10, then cross out the tens to produce *c* = 25. Celebrate their wonderful ideas with them. Assign math partners and pass out a recording sheet (Appendix J) to each pair of children.

☀ Introduce the foreign coins investigation and have children determine the value of coin *c*.

Behind the Numbers

It is intentional that the fourth mystery coin, *y*, has been given two clues ($y + 5 = 10$ and $y + y + 10 = 5 + 5 + 5 + y$). The first clue is likely to engender an undoing strategy—what plus five produces ten is likely to be solved as ten minus five. On the other hand, the second clue is likely to be solved by "cancellation" and equivalence. The two clues have been juxtaposed to provide a chance for children to consider both strategies—undoing (subtracting five) and using equivalence.

Supporting the Investigation

☀ Make note of children's strategies as they work to figure out the values of the other foreign coins.

As children work on the foreign coin investigation, walk around and take note of the strategies you see. Confer with children as needed to support and challenge their investigations. Note especially whether they are developing a variety of strategies to help them solve for unknowns.

Conferring with Children at Work

Inside One Classroom

Author's Notes

Jasmine: This one *(referring to Coin x)* is hard.

Trish (the teacher): It is, isn't it! That's what makes it fun, too, though. Right? Easy ones are boring, I think. Hmm…how should we start? What do you think, Heather? Any ideas?

Heather: *(Shrugs.)* I think it must be in the middle of 20 and 40 somewhere.

Trish: Let's draw a number line.

Jasmine: Where do we put *x*, though? We don't know what it is.

Trish: What do we know? Do we know anything about the size of the jumps?

Jasmine: They are the same size but we don't know how big.

Trish: Well, let's draw that. *(Writes:)*

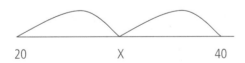

20   X   40

Trish confers like a fellow mathematician. By commenting on the fun of doing difficult problems, she models how mathematicians enjoy puzzlement. She acknowledges that this problem is difficult and does not make the children feel that this is a test item and that they are being asked to figure out an answer that she already knows. Instead, she supports their work as mathematicians. She respects children's autonomy and trusts them to generate clever solutions.

Mathematicians often begin by establishing what is known and thinking about how to model it.

Using the number line, Trish represents what the children say they know.

Continued on next page

Jasmine: We land on 20 and 40. Hey!! It is in the middle. It must be 30.

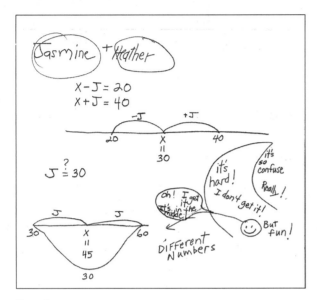

Figure 2

Assessment Tips

This is a good moment to take stock of which children can now easily use strategies such as "canceling" and substitution, and which children may still be trying to do arithmetic. What strategies do they use today to solve for unknowns? Continue to use the graphic of the landscape of learning and color in the landmarks for each child that you have evidence for. Use sticky notes to make comments on their work and place today's work in their portfolios.

Preparing for the Math Congress

After children have had ample time to work on the problems in Appendix J, ask them to prepare for today's math congress by making a list of the strategies they found most helpful. You will probably see several strategies such as the following on their lists, although they may invent their own terminology to describe them:

❖ crossing out ("cancellation")

❖ trading (using equivalence and substituting)

❖ making a picture on the open double number line

❖ undoing ($y + 5 = 10$ can be solved as $y = 10 - 5$)

> ☀ Ask children to make a list of the strategies they found most helpful in solving the foreign coins problems.

Facilitating the Math Congress

☀ Structure a discussion around the strategies children used and then shift the conversation to how the strategies are related.

Structure the congress as a discussion of each strategy and where it was the most helpful. Then shift the conversation to how the strategies are related. For example, the undoing strategy eliminates the +5 by adding –5 to each side of the equation. As the children share the strategies they have developed for solving for unknowns, post their ideas on a "strategy wall" and celebrate the children's wonderful accomplishments.

Reflections on the Day

Today children continued to explore equations as they solved for unknowns. Determining whether statements were true or not, they learned the importance of examining the special case of $n = 0$. As they worked to solve for unknowns, they used many strategies that were developed as this unit progressed: the commutative and associative properties, "cancellation" and substitution, equivalence, and undoing. Most important, instead of automatically resorting to arithmetic procedures, children are beginning to see equivalent expressions as objects that can be operated on.

DAY EIGHT
Subways

The context of subways in New York City, taken from the story *The Masloppy Family Goes to New York City,* is used to introduce children to input and output, net change, and systematic ways to organize and generate all possibilities. The entire math workshop today will be devoted to carrying out this investigation.

Day Eight Outline

Developing the Context

☀ Introduce the context of keeping track of passengers getting on and off a subway.

Supporting the Investigation

☀ Note children's strategies as they work on the investigation.

☀ Help them to realize that there are several possibilities and encourage them to figure out a way to keep track.

Preparing for the Math Congress

☀ Plan to highlight a variety of representations and strategies during the math congress.

Facilitating the Math Congress

☀ Record children's solutions and question whether the class has found all the possibilities.

☀ Do not show children a way to keep track, but if children have noticed patterns, let them share their ideas.

Materials Needed

The Masloppy Family Goes to New York City (Appendix A)

Large chart paper—one sheet per pair of children

Large chart pad and easel

Markers

Developing the Context

☀ Introduce the context of keeping track of passengers getting on and off a subway.

Remind children of the story *The Masloppy Family Goes to New York City.* Ask them if they remember the three trips that Nicholas and his family planned in the city and if necessary reread the section that describes the trips. One of the trips—the one Nicholas wanted—was to ride on subways and go to the Empire State Building. Ask the children if they have ever been on a subway. Have them describe the experience and then talk about the way that people get on and off at each station stop.

Tell them you are picturing Nicholas in New York City, on the subway. Since he loves to organize, he'll probably be trying to count all the people getting on and off the train. But it all happens so fast! There isn't time to count.

Picture with the class a scenario of ten people, including you, on the train as it pulls out of the station. At the next stop some people may have boarded and some may have left the train. But when the train pulls out of the station you counted fifteen people on the train, so something happened! Pose the following questions:

> *If there were ten people on the train and one person left and now there are fifteen, how many must have gotten on? But perhaps not only one person left? The only thing I know for certain is that I stayed on.*

Ask children to work with their math partners and be organizers like Nicholas. Ask them to figure out all the possibilities of what might have happened:

> *How many people could have left the train and how many could have boarded it if first there were ten and now there are fifteen and I stayed on?*

Supporting the Investigation

☀ Note children's strategies as they work on the investigation.

☀ Help them to realize that there are several possibilities and encourage them to figure out a way to keep track.

Distribute large chart paper to each pair of children. As they work, walk around and take note of the strategies you see. Sit and confer with pairs of children as they work. Most of the children are likely to realize that there are multiple solutions, but they may not realize that the number of solutions is finite; also they may not be approaching the finding of solutions systematically. As you confer with these children, ask them how many possibilities they think there are. (There are exactly ten, including the possibility of no one leaving the train and five additional passengers getting on.) Wonder with them if there might be a way to keep track of the possibilities they have found. Remind them that Nicholas is an organizer and he would no doubt seek a way to organize the possibilities. Note the different ways children find and represent their solutions. You will probably see diagrams and pictures, number lines, prose, and equations. A few children may think there is only one solution. As you confer with them you might ask, "What if two people left the train?" or "What if twelve people got on?" Questions like these will help them realize there are several possibilities.

Sample Children's Work

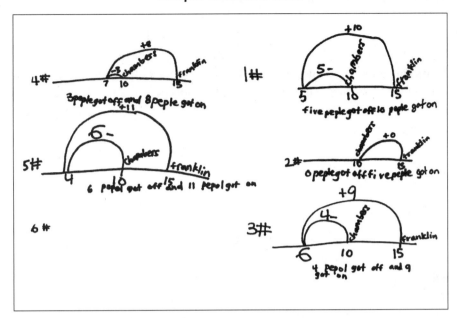

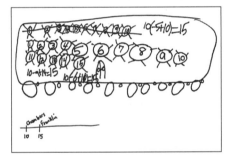
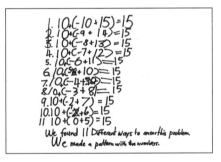

Preparing for the Math Congress

After the children have devoted a sufficient amount of time to the investigation, ask them to prepare for a math congress. Since they have been working on large chart paper and you will be doing a similar investigation on Day Nine, it is not necessary to ask children to make posters. Just ask them to prepare to share their strategies, the possibilities they have found, and the ways they are keeping track. Note the different ways children are representing and organizing their work. Are any of them beginning to think about a system—decreasing by one the number leaving the train and then decreasing by one the number boarding the train? Are any starting at $-9 + 14$ and proceeding systematically to $-8 + 13$, $-7 + 12$, etc.? Do you hear any children talking about a pattern? These various ways of keeping track of the possibilities will make for a rich conversation in the math congress.

Do not expect that many children will have found all ten possibilities or that they will have discussed the net gain (+5) or the equivalence in the solutions, for example, $-9 + 14 = -8 + 13$. Over the next two days they will be exploring this situation further and as their work becomes more systematic these ideas will arise naturally.

☀ Plan to highlight a variety of representations and strategies during the math congress.

Facilitating the Math Congress

☀ Record children's solutions and question whether the class has found all the possibilities.

☀ Do not show children a way to keep track, but if children have noticed patterns, let them share their ideas.

You will probably find it helpful to use this congress to discuss a variety of solutions. Several children can share solutions they found and you can record them. This will help children who think there are only a few solutions to realize that there are many more. Wonder aloud how many solutions there might be and if the class has found them all. Ask if anyone found a good way to keep track. Do *not* show children a systematic way to keep track. Let the children be the mathematicians. If any children have started a systematic approach, let them share it.

▪ Assessment Tips

Collect the work completed today and make notes regarding the children's approaches. Over the next two days you might expect to see changes in their ability to work systematically, in their ability to prove they have all the possibilities, and in their understanding of the equivalence in their solutions and its relationship to net gain. By collecting the work today and analyzing it, you can chart each child's growth and development.

Reflections on the Day

Today children began a new investigation and explored several new mathematical ideas: how to examine input and output systematically, how to determine and use net change, how to recognize that a variety of solutions are all equivalent, and how to know and prove that all solutions have been found. Today you laid the groundwork for these ideas. Over the next two days children will have opportunities to develop them.

DAY NINE
Subways

The context of subways in New York City from the story *The Masloppy Family Goes to New York City* is used again to provide children with more opportunities to explore input and output, net change, and systematic ways to organize and generate all possibilities. The entire math workshop is again devoted to this investigation.

Day Nine Outline

Developing the Context

* Remind children of their investigation on Day Eight and introduce a new subway scenario.

* Suggest that children find a way to be sure they have all the possible solutions.

Supporting the Investigation

* Note whether children are working more systematically than they did on Day Eight.

Preparing for the Math Congress

* Plan for a math congress that will highlight all the possibilities children found and some of their more systematic approaches to keeping track.

Facilitating the Math Congress

* As children share their solutions, challenge them to convince their classmates that they have found all the possibilities.

Students' work from Day Eight

Large chart paper— one sheet per pair of children

Markers

Developing the Context

☀ Remind children of their investigation on Day Eight and introduce a new subway scenario.

☀ Suggest that children find a way to be sure they have all the possible solutions.

Remind the children of the investigation they did on Day Eight about what happened at a subway stop. Explain that they will investigate another subway scenario today. This time there were ten people on board when the train pulled in, just as on Day Eight, but when the train pulled out there were seventeen people on it. Ask:

If no one left the train, how many passengers must have gotten on?

If some of the children began to work systematically on Day Eight, remind them of that work and post it. Assign math partners and ask them to find a good way to organize their work today. Suggest that they try to find a way to be sure that they have all the possible solutions for the question:

How many people could have left the train and how many could have gotten on, if before the stop there were ten aboard, and after the stop there are seventeen, and I stayed on?

Supporting the Investigation

☀ Note whether children are working more systematically than they did on Day Eight.

As children work, walk around and take note of the strategies you see. Sit and confer with children as they work. Today everyone is likely to know that there are multiple solutions, and you should see more organization of the possible solutions. Ask children how many possibilities they think there are and if they think there will be more than on Day Eight. (There are exactly ten again. The net gain is different, + 7 versus + 5, but no more than nine passengers can leave the train because you stayed on and there are only ten passengers on the train to start. It is also possible that no one left, which is the tenth possibility.) Encourage children to keep track of the number of possibilities they find. Wonder with them if there might be a way to organize their work so they'll know for certain that they have found all the solutions. Remind them again that Nicholas was an organizer and he would seek a way to organize the possibilities. Suggest they work like Nicholas. Note the different ways children find and represent their solutions today and if they are working more systematically. If some children approach the task with a random search, you can encourage them to continue looking by commenting that another pair of children found six possibilities, or ten. With pairs of children who work systematically to find all ten possibilities, you can propose that maybe there is still one more possible solution. You may thus encourage them to try to prove to you that your suggested eleventh solution is not possible.

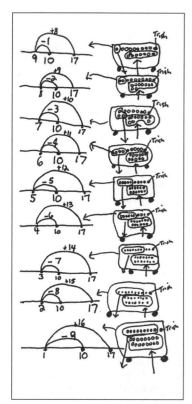

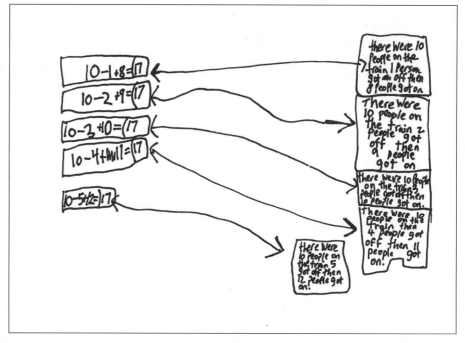

Conferring with Children at Work (Tova and Haille)

Inside One Classroom

Author's Notes

Tova: We figured out it was easier to minus first. *(They have used the number line and started with 10 and jumped back, then forward. They have started with 10 − 5 + 12. Although they have worked systematically, they have found only five possibilities since they stopped at 10 − 9 + 16.)* We did it like this: first 5 got off, then 6, then 7, then 8, then 9. Ten can't get off because you stayed on to count.

Trish joins the children at work and lets them share their excitement about their new approach.

Trish (the teacher): I see you are really organizing today. Subtracting first is a great idea. Yesterday when you were adding first, it was hard to keep track, wasn't it, and you added too many. *(Yesterday they had produced some situations like 30 getting on and 25 getting off).* Do you think you have all the possibilities?

Trish celebrates this new accomplishment and clarifies why it is helping them. Then she challenges, "Do you have them all?"

Haille: Well, we can't think of any more, but they've got more than us *(pointing to the girls next to them)* so we are still looking.

Trish: Let's see, you started at minus 5 and went all the way down to minus 9. Could you extend your pattern in the other direction?

Trish starts with the strategy the children are using and guides them with a question.

Tova: Oh, now I see! *(They get more paper and tape it to the top of their sheet and then continue upward with 10 − 4 + 11).*

It's OK if drafts are messy. Using tape is fine. These are young mathematicians at work.

Inside One Classroom

Author's Notes

Chynna: We have them all. See.

Austin: Yep. Minus 9, minus 7, minus 1, minus 6…and all these, too.

Trish (the teacher): And are you sure that you have them all?

Although Austin and Chynna have found all the possibilities, Trish wants to challenge them to prove that they have them all.

Austin: *(Looking a little uncertain.)* We think so.

Trish: Hmmm…Oh, I think I know one more.

Chynna: Really? Let's find it, Austin. I want to have all of them.

Trish: I'll check back with you in a little while, OK? …*(Returning later.)* What did you decide? Did you find it?

Chynna: No. We think you made a mistake and we can prove it! See. You can't leave the train so we have to start with 9 off the train, then 8…and you keep going to zero—no one gets off the train. It's one person less every time…so we know none are missing.

After Trish left, they organized their work and used a system to check carefully. As they worked, they developed a certainty that there could be no more possibilities.

Trish: Hmm…you convinced me. I must have made a mistake.

Austin: Yeah! *(Said with a big smile.)*

The children own the justification and they celebrate that they have convinced Trish. Crafting a justification and knowing with certainty that you have solved the problem is where the exhilaration of doing mathematics comes from!

Preparing for the Math Congress

☀ Plan for a math congress that will highlight all the possibilities children found and some of their more systematic approaches to keeping track.

After a sufficient amount of time has been devoted to the investigation, ask the children to prepare for a congress. As on Day Eight, since they have been working on large chart paper and you will be doing a similar investigation on Day Ten, it is not necessary to ask the children to make posters. Just ask them to prepare to share their strategies, the possibilities they have found, the ways they are keeping track, and in particular their reasons for thinking they have found all the possibilities—and to come prepared to prove it. Note the different ways children are representing and organizing their work. You should see more organized work today. Perhaps several children are now beginning to think about a system—decreasing by one the number of subway riders leaving the train and then decreasing by one the number of passengers getting on, $-9 + 16$, $-8 + 15$, etc. Are any children starting at $0 + 7$ and proceeding systematically to $-1 + 8$, $-2 + 9$, etc.? Do you hear any of those children who, on Day Eight, worked randomly, today talking about a pattern? In the upcoming congress, you will want to focus on how many possibilities the children found and their proofs for how they can know that they have them all.

■ Tips for Structuring the Math Congress

Since the focus of this congress will be on ways to organize the solutions and proofs that all the possibilities have been found, look for pairs of children who have produced samples of work such as the following:

❖ A pair that has begun a systematic approach even if they have not found all the possibilities. In congress, the community can help such children to extend the pattern and find the possibilities that are missing.

❖ A pair that has begun by removing 9, then 8, then 7, etc. (removing one fewer passenger each time).

❖ A pair that has begun by removing no passengers, then 1, then 2, etc. (removing one more passenger each time).

After each pair shares, ask them to convince the community that they have found all the possibilities. One form of proof in mathematics is "proof by all cases." Listen to the children's language as they defend their thinking. Note if they argue that no more than nine can ever leave the train because you must stay on and because they have proceeded systematically (adding or subtracting one each time) they know that there are no other possibilities. If you have pairs of children whose work fits the last two descriptions listed above, you can use their examples to explore how both approaches work, and you can ask the community to find the possibilities on the charts that are similar (as illustrated in Inside One Classroom, page 60).

Facilitating the Math Congress

Convene the children in the meeting area. Bring the two or three charts you will use for discussion. Ask the pairs one at a time to explain their strategies. Encourage comments and questions on each. Challenge each pair to convince the community that they have found all the possibilities. After each pair has shared, ask the community if the proof they offered is convincing, and why or why not.

☀ As children share their solutions, challenge them to convince their classmates that they have found all the possibilities.

A Portion of the Math Congress

Trish (the teacher): Devin and Philip and Ava and Danielle, when you shared, you both described a system—a pattern that helped you…but your systems were different. Let's post your work and look at it. *(Both charts are taped up on the chalkboard for the community to examine).* First, did they convince you that they have all the possibilities? Maybe they have different ones?

Isaac: I think they have different ones. Devin and Philip have 10 minus 2 plus 9. Ava and Danielle have "Nine people got on the train and 2 people left." *(Referring to 10 + 9 − 2.)*

Mia Chiara: It's the same thing, just put a different way.

Isaac: Oh, yeah. It's like an input and output machine! And they convinced me because they used a pattern. They found all the ways. Devin and Philip took people off first and then added. Ava and Danielle added the people first and then took some out.

Author's Notes

Trish does not affirm the "correctness" of solutions. Doing so may hinder thinking as children just accept the "wisdom of the teacher" as the "knowing one." Instead she asks the community to consider the work of these mathematicians and to determine if the strategies have produced different possibilities. She is challenging children to think, to examine equivalence and the proofs.

Sample Children's Work

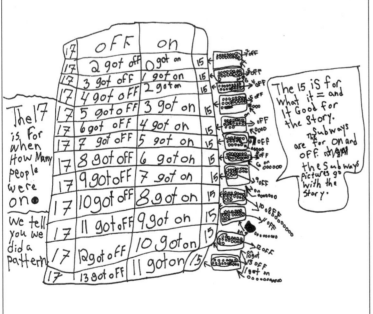

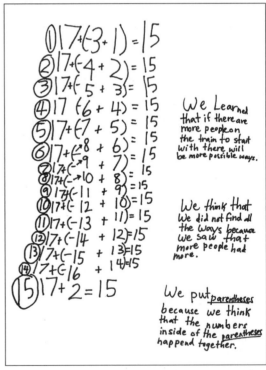

▨ Assessment Tips

Collect the completed work today and make notes regarding the children's approaches. Compare the work to that completed on Day Eight. Note growth and development in the children's abilities to work more systematically. Using the graphic of the landscape of learning, continue to map out children's pathways. Do you have evidence for each child? On Day Ten you will have a chance to observe again as children continue to work on net change.

Reflections on the Day

Children continued to work on ways to examine input and output systematically and on how to know and justify concluding that all solutions have been found. On Day Ten they will continue this work, but with a focus on net change and equivalence.

DAY TEN
Subways

Materials Needed

Students' work from
Days Eight and Nine

Large chart paper—
one sheet per pair
of children

Markers

The context of subways in New York City from the story *The Masloppy Family Goes to New York City* is used again to provide children with a further opportunity to explore input and output, net gain and loss, and systematic ways to organize and generate all possible solutions. The entire math workshop is again devoted to this investigation, but this time the focus is on net change and the total number of possibilities.

Day Ten Outline

Developing the Context

☀ Introduce the final subway scenario and ask children if they think they will find more or fewer possibilities than in the previous two investigations.

☀ Encourage children to look for patterns in the data as they work.

Supporting the Investigation

☀ Encourage children to keep track of the number of possibilities they find.

Preparing for the Math Congress

☀ Plan a math congress focused on how many possibilities the children found, whether this is more or fewer than in previous investigations, and on any new patterns they have noticed.

Facilitating the Math Congress

☀ Ask children to explain the patterns they have noticed and encourage a focus on net change.

Developing the Context

Remind the children of the work they did on Day Nine investigating what happened at a subway stop. Explain that you have yet one more subway scenario to investigate today. When the train left the stop on Day Nine, there were seventeen people on it. At the next stop there was a flurry of activity again and then when the train departed there were only fifteen people. Pose the following scenario:

> *The number of passengers went from seventeen to fifteen. What happened?*

Ask children if they think they will find more possibilities than before or fewer. Remind them of the wonderful patterns they found helpful on Day Nine and ask them to keep looking during today's investigation—perhaps they will find more patterns. Perhaps there is even a way to know before beginning how many possibilities there will be. Remind them that as before you stayed on the train. Assign math partners, distribute chart paper, and let the children begin working.

Supporting the Investigation

As children work, walk around and take note of the strategies you see. Sit and confer with pairs of children as they work. Today most children will probably proceed with a systematic approach. Ask them how many possibilities they think there are and if they think there will be more or fewer than on Day Nine. Encourage children to keep track of the number of possibilities they find.

Preparing for the Math Congress

After children have had a sufficient amount of time to work on the problem, ask them to prepare for a math congress. Since they have been working on large chart paper, it is not necessary to ask them to make posters. Just ask them to prepare to discuss how many possibilities they found and any new patterns they have noticed. In the math congress today, you will want to focus on how many possibilities they found, a comparison of this amount to the amounts found on the previous two days, and any new patterns they have noticed, such as net change.

☀ Introduce the final subway scenario and ask children if they think they will find more or fewer possibilities than in the previous two investigations.

☀ Encourage children to look for patterns in the data as they work.

Behind the Numbers

The net change here, –2, has been designed to be small and to be a loss. Children are likely to think there will be few possibilities because the difference is so small. But in fact there are more possibilities, because fifteen people were on the train originally. On the other days this context was discussed, there were only ten. There are exactly fifteen possibilities today. The net change is –2. The greatest number of passengers that can leave is sixteen. The least number that can leave is two. The choice of numbers is likely to cause children to ponder, Why are there more possibilities? Can I know before listing them how many possibilities there will be? Is there a relationship between the number of people on the train at the start and the number of possibilities? Is each of the possibilities always an equivalent expression to the net change?

☀ Encourage children to keep track of the number of possibilities they find.

☀ Plan a math congress focused on how many possibilities the children found, whether this is more or fewer than in previous investigations, and on any new patterns they have noticed.

Tips for Structuring the Math Congress

Since the focus of this congress will be on net change and other new observations, look for pairs of children who have produced samples of work such as the following:

❖ A pair of children that has noticed that the net change is always –2. In congress, the community can look back at the other subway situations (Days Eight and Nine) and consider the net change found in the problems examined on those days.

❖ A pair that has noticed that the number of possibilities is related to the number of people on the train originally. In the congress the community can look back at the data from the other days and compare the number of possibilities to the number of people on the train.

❖ A pair that has begun to look at the result of the actions of boarding and leaving as objects (equivalent expressions): $-16 + 14 = -15 + 13$, etc.

Be aware that the associative property holds for addition, but it does not hold for subtraction. For example:

$$(15 + 2) + 3 = 15 + (2 + 3)$$
$$\text{But } (15 - 2) - 3 \text{ is not equivalent to } 15 - (2 - 3).$$

For this reason, be careful how you use parentheses. You might also be tempted to use parentheses to help children focus on the action. The notation below is not correct either, since it is read to mean seventeen multiplied by the number in the parentheses.

$$17(-16 + 14)$$

Although you need to be careful in your use of notation, think twice before you correct children's notation. Formal notation at this point in development can hinder children's sense-making. They often use incorrect notation because they are representing action. For example, the poster made by Austin and Isaac (page 65) has strings of equations which, given order of operations rules, are technically incorrect (addition must be done before subtraction), and yet the thinking on the poster is beautiful. The boys are representing people leaving a train and people boarding and it would make no sense to tell them that addition must be done first! You could tell them that the equation should be written as $17 + (-16 + 14)$, indicating that what is inside the parentheses is done first, but does this match the children's thinking? In fact, it is likely to get in the way of their sense-making because they are thinking about some of the seventeen people getting off the train; they are not thinking of the –16 as an integer. Sometimes it is important and helpful to introduce children to formal notation, but you have to be very careful in determining when this is appropriate. Just as invented spelling is welcomed in the early years of language arts instruction as children begin to isolate phonemes and represent them, children's informal notation in mathematics can represent the emergence of powerful ideas.

Facilitating the Math Congress

Convene the children in the meeting area. Bring the two or three charts you will have chosen for discussion. Ask the pairs one at a time to explain the patterns they have noticed. Encourage comments and questions on each.

☀ Ask children to explain the patterns they have noticed and encourage a focus on net change.

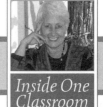

A Portion of the Math Congress

Inside One Classroom

Austin and Isaac have just shared their poster and children are commenting.

$$17 - 2 = 15 \quad 17 - 14 + 12 = 15$$
$$17 - 3 + 1 = 15 \quad 17 - 15 + 13 = 15$$
$$17 - 4 + 2 = 15 \quad 17 - 16 + 14 = 15$$
$$17 - 5 + 3 = 15$$
$$17 - 6 + 4 = 15$$
$$17 - 7 + 5 = 15$$
$$17 - 8 + 6 = 15$$
$$17 - 9 + 7 = 15$$
$$17 - 10 + 8 = 15$$
$$17 - 11 + 9 = 15$$
$$17 - 12 + 10 = 15$$
$$17 - 13 + 11 = 15$$

We can4 have eny more becuase you can't take away 17. why not? becuase you only have 17. Oh. there is a patern. how is there a patern?

The minis begins at 2. The plus begins at 1. I Don't get it! OK so if you look closly you will sort of see it going like 1,2,3,4,5,6,7,8,9. how do you get it. Wow! now I get it.

Author's Notes

The dialogue ball is very interesting here. It is bouncing from child to child to child with little need for Trish to comment. This is evidence of a real community hard at work trying to understand.

Devin: The number that minuses has to be two numbers bigger than the number that plusses.

Mia Chiara: On every one, it minuses 2.

Rosie: Two got off, zero got on. That equals 2. All the way down on both sides it's always 2.

Trish (the teacher): Do you mean it is always minus 2?

Continued on next page

Continued from previous page

Sam: Yes. The difference. But the numbers are two more than the other side, too—4 is two more than 2, 7 is two more than 5.

Aidan: It's 3 and 1, 4 and 2, 5 and 3, 6 and 4. It's like counting by twos but using the numbers in between.

Trish: Say more about that, Aidan.

Net change is a challenging idea and the children are working hard to understand it.

Juanita: I know what he means. Everything is two away. If 4 got off, 2 got on because it's 2 away from the number you started with.

Michael: Each time two more people left than got on.

Trish: You have been making some important observations. Are there any questions for Austin and Isaac?

Austin: I have a question myself. I get that they go in order, and the minus is more than the plus. So if you take away more, do you add less?

Keshawn: If you add less you won't get to the right number.

Austin and Keshawn are grappling with the idea of equivalence here. How is it possible that the net loss stays constant?

Jasmine: Because 15 is two less than 17.

Haille: Because 17 is two more than 15. If you're taking away more, you're ending up with less.

Chynna: And 17 minus 2 equals 15. So I think that relates to the other question, why off is two more than on.

Mia Chiara: I don't fully understand. It has to do with the pattern: one getting higher, the other getting lower.

Michael: What Chynna is trying to say and what Haille is trying to say is that everything you do, it has to have two more people getting off the train than getting on it.

The work of generalizing gets to the heart of algebra.

▉ Assessment Tips

Collect the work completed today and make notes regarding the children's approaches. Compare the work to what they completed on Days Eight and Nine. Think about the math congress and the generalizations children made about net change. Note further growth and development in children's ability to work systematically. Continue to map out each child's pathways on the graphic of the landscape of learning; you should now have evidence for everyone.

TRADES, JUMPS, AND STOPS

Reflections on the Unit

In algebra, one symbol (*x*, for example) can mean many things. That's why we call it a variable. But when we set up an equation with mathematical symbols, the relationships represented are specific. The definition of the variable is also specific. The mathematician Georg Lichtenberg expressed this power of algebraic language well when he wrote, "In mathematical analysis we call *x* the undetermined part of line *a:* the rest we don't call *y*, as we do in common life, but *a − x.* Hence mathematical language has great advantages over the common language" (Woodard 2000). The symbols used in algebra are defined in relationship to one another. And this gets right to the heart of mathematics—the describing and quantifying of relationships.

In your community of young mathematicians at work, big ideas and strategies on the landscape of learning for algebra are under construction. In this unit children have explored relationships and equivalence in many ways. They have analyzed equations, represented equivalent expressions on the number line, investigated variables, solved for unknowns, and developed strategies for simplifying equations such as "canceling," substituting, and undoing. They have examined and used the associative and commutative properties for addition. They have been introduced to proof and have been encouraged to justify and convince. Most important, they have been supported throughout this unit in generalizing, in noticing patterns and relationships, and in building ideas for themselves. All these ideas and strategies are the foundation for the more advanced mathematical work they will do in later years.

U p a big, big hill, down a long, long path, through a thick, thick forest, there is an old, old house.

This is the house of the Masloppy family.

Inside there is a big, big staircase. It twists and twists all through the house. It goes by the rooms of Delia and Petula, to the rooms of Henrietta and Violet, past the rooms of Uncle Lloyd and Grandma Eudora, and then to the room of Baby Oscar.

It even goes to the doghouse of Itchy.

At the very tip-top of the staircase is the room of Nicholas, the Organizer. Nicholas is seven. He was nicknamed the Organizer because he likes to organize things. Once he helped his family organize everything in the house. He even helped Uncle Lloyd organize all his T-shirts in piles of five, and that had started Grandma Eudora thinking about starting the Masloppy T-Shirt Factory.

But tonight Nicholas was not organizing anything. He was sitting outside his room on the tippety-top step of the staircase. He was waiting and waiting. Delia was there waiting, too. She was sitting on the stairs with Petula, Violet, Henrietta, and Baby Oscar. Even Itchy was there waiting, waiting, waiting . . .

They were all waiting because tonight was the special night—the night they got to open up the big piggy bank to see how much money was in it!

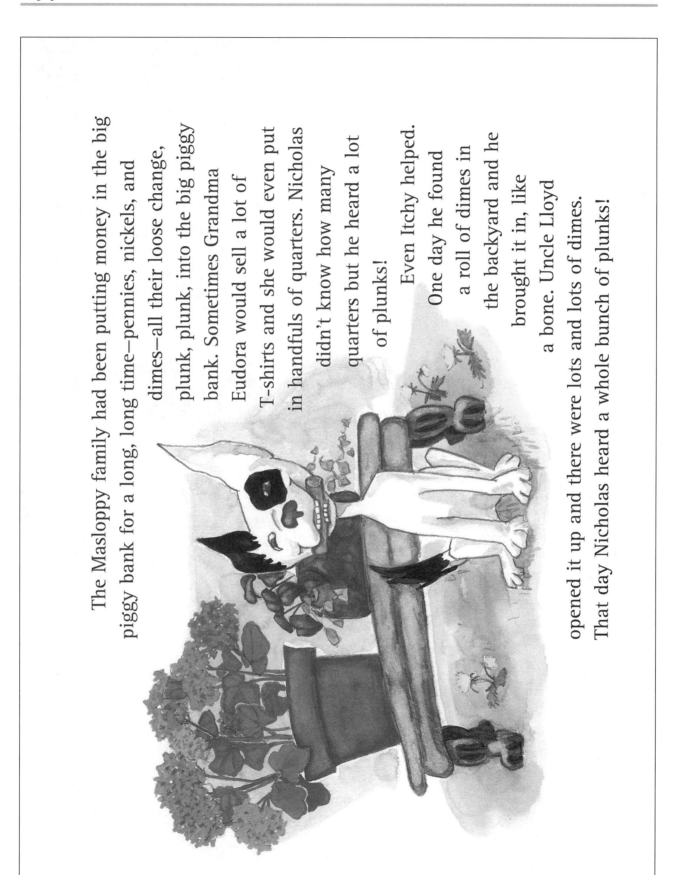

The Masloppy family had been putting money in the big piggy bank for a long, long time—pennies, nickels, and dimes—all their loose change, plunk, plunk, into the big piggy bank. Sometimes Grandma Eudora would sell a lot of T-shirts and she would even put in handfuls of quarters. Nicholas didn't know how many quarters but he heard a lot of plunks!

Even Itchy helped. One day he found a roll of dimes in the backyard and he brought it in, like a bone. Uncle Lloyd opened it up and there were lots and lots of dimes. That day Nicholas heard a whole bunch of plunks!

Sometimes Henrietta and Nicholas would try to shake the big piggy bank. It would jingle and jingle. They wondered how much was in it but they couldn't tell because the money was all inside and there was no way to even peek.

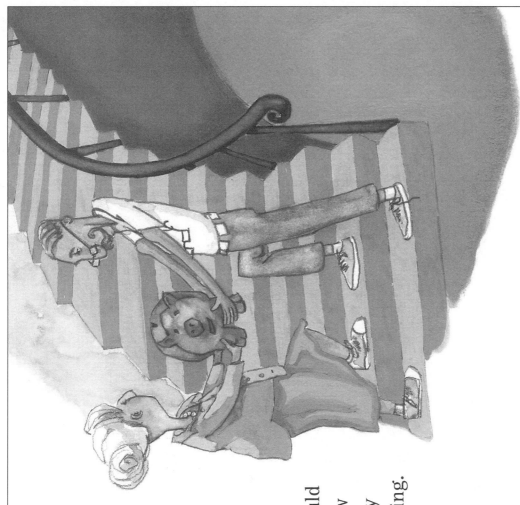

But now the piggy bank didn't jingle and it didn't plunk. It was full. No more coins could fit! Uncle Lloyd and Grandma Eudora were going to open the big piggy bank tonight and if there was enough money in it the family would all go on a vacation to New York City! And so here they all sat waiting and wondering. Would there be enough?

Soon they heard Grandma Eudora and Uncle Lloyd coming up the steps with the piggy bank. They all ran to Nicholas's room and Uncle Lloyd and Grandma Eudora came in carrying the big piggy bank. It was so heavy it took the two of them to carry it! They placed it in the middle of the floor. Grandma Eudora took a small key out of her pocket and put it into the keyhole on the side of the piggy bank. At first the key seemed stuck, but then she turned it and the bank opened. A huge, huge pile of coins spilled to the floor—quarters, nickels, dimes, and pennies. Lots and lots and lots! Baby Oscar clapped his hands in glee and Itchy did backflips. "How shall we ever count all this?" Henrietta exclaimed.

Violet and Delia gasped.

"I have an idea," Nicholas said. "We can organize it. We'll sort it and put the coins in wrappers and make rolls like the roll Itchy found."

Itchy liked that idea and he barked to show his excitement.

"We'll do the pennies," Violet and Henrietta offered.

"OK. We'll do the dimes," Delia and Petula said.

Uncle Lloyd and Grandma Eudora started to sort the nickels and quarters while Nicholas ran to get wrappers. First they put all the quarters in piles of four, because four quarters make a dollar.

When Nicholas came back, they looked at the wrappers. The wrappers for the quarters were marked $10. "How many quarters is that?" Nicholas wondered. He began to skip-count. "Four, eight, twelve, sixteen, twenty. Twenty quarters in five piles. That makes five dollars. If twenty quarters make five dollars, then I think we need forty quarters to make ten dollars." Nicholas counted out forty quarters, ten piles of four, and rolled them. He hoped he was right.

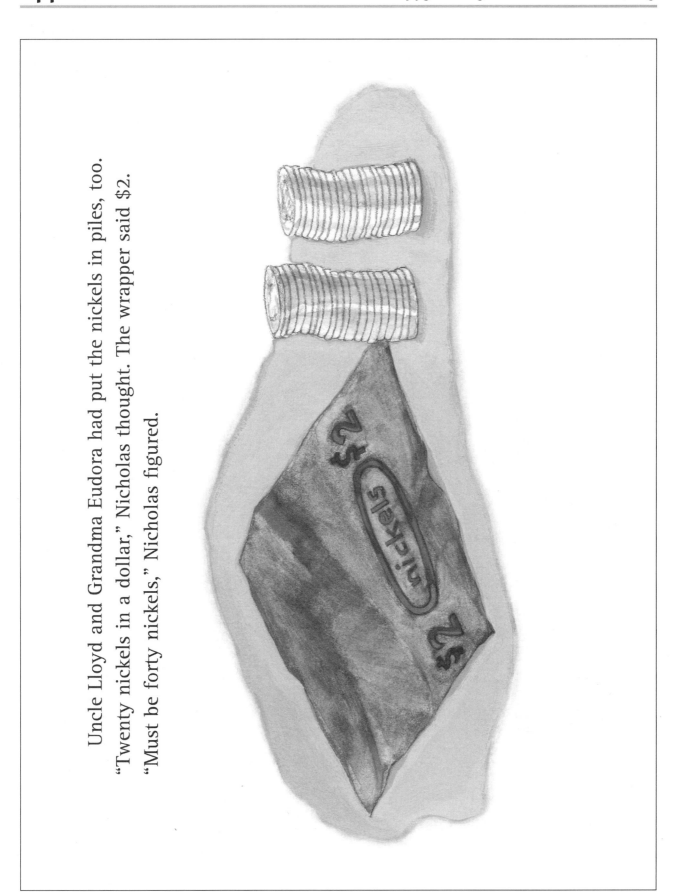

Uncle Lloyd and Grandma Eudora had put the nickels in piles, too. "Twenty nickels in a dollar," Nicholas thought. The wrapper said $2. "Must be forty nickels," Nicholas figured.

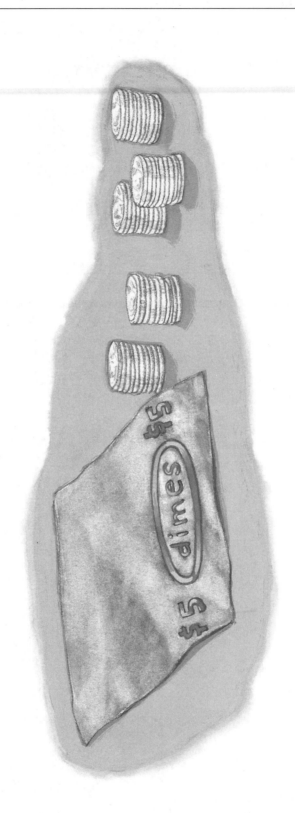

Delia and Petula made piles with ten dimes in each, because ten dimes make a dollar. The dimes wrapper said $5. They put five piles in it and rolled them up. "How many dimes was that?" Delia wondered as she rolled the five piles up in the wrapper.

Violet and Henrietta rolled the pennies—fifty cents in each roll.

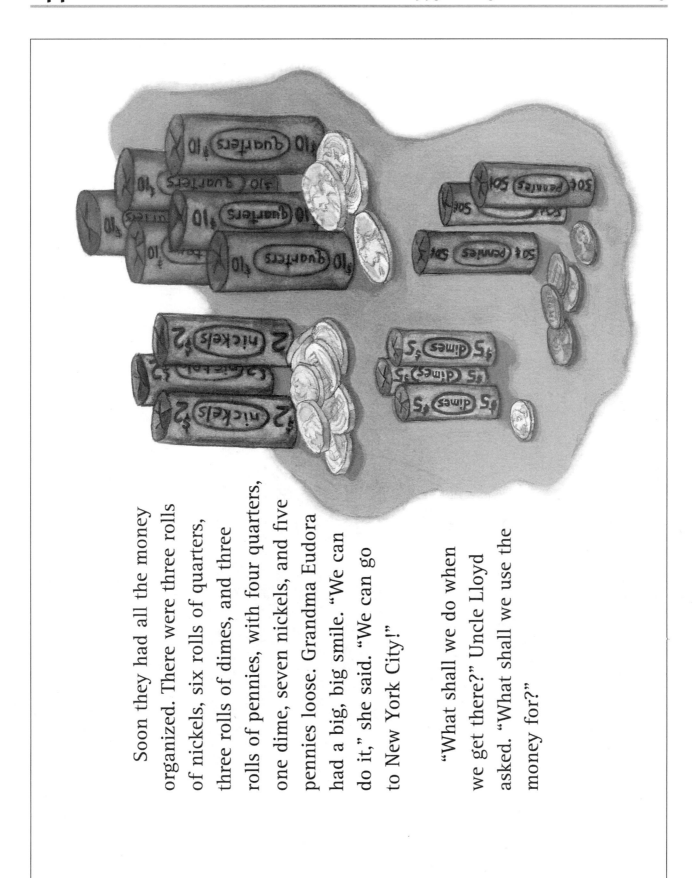

Soon they had all the money organized. There were three rolls of nickels, six rolls of quarters, three rolls of dimes, and three rolls of pennies, with four quarters, one dime, seven nickels, and five pennies loose. Grandma Eudora had a big, big smile. "We can do it," she said. "We can go to New York City!"

"What shall we do when we get there?" Uncle Lloyd asked. "What shall we use the money for?"

"We want to see the dinosaurs at the Museum of Natural History!" Henrietta and Violet exclaimed, jumping up and down.

"The boat ride! The boat ride around the city!" Delia and Petula yelled, clapping their hands and running in circles around Nicholas's room. Baby Oscar clapped his hands, too!

"I want to go to the bottom and to the top of the city!" Nicholas announced. "I want to go on the subways underground and then to the very top of the Empire State Building to see the whole city."

"We'll do it all," Uncle Lloyd said, laughing. "Nicholas, sort the money into three piles for us: one pile for the museum trip to see the dinosaurs, one pile for the boat ride, and one pile for the subways and the Empire State Building."

So Nicholas did. He made three equivalent piles and put each in a bag. Then he tied a big bow with ribbon around each bag and made three signs. One sign said Boat Trip. Another said, Dinosaurs, and the third said, Subway and the Empire State Building.

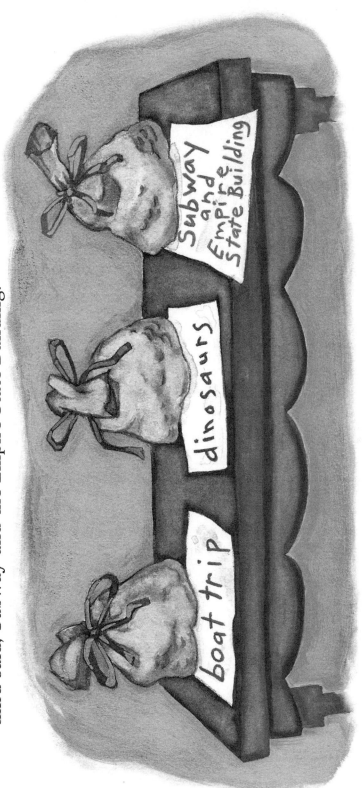

"Now let the trips begin!" Nicholas announced with a big grin. "We are organized and ready!"

Names _____ Date _____

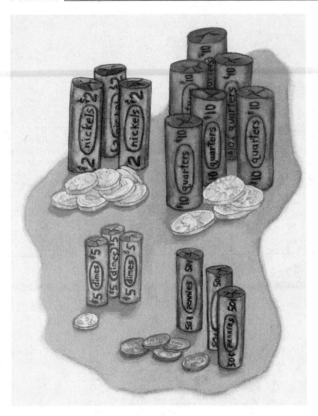

This is what we think is in the bags:

For the museum trip:

For the boat trip:

For the subway and Empire State Building:

■ The cards can be made more durable by pasting them on oaktag and laminating them.

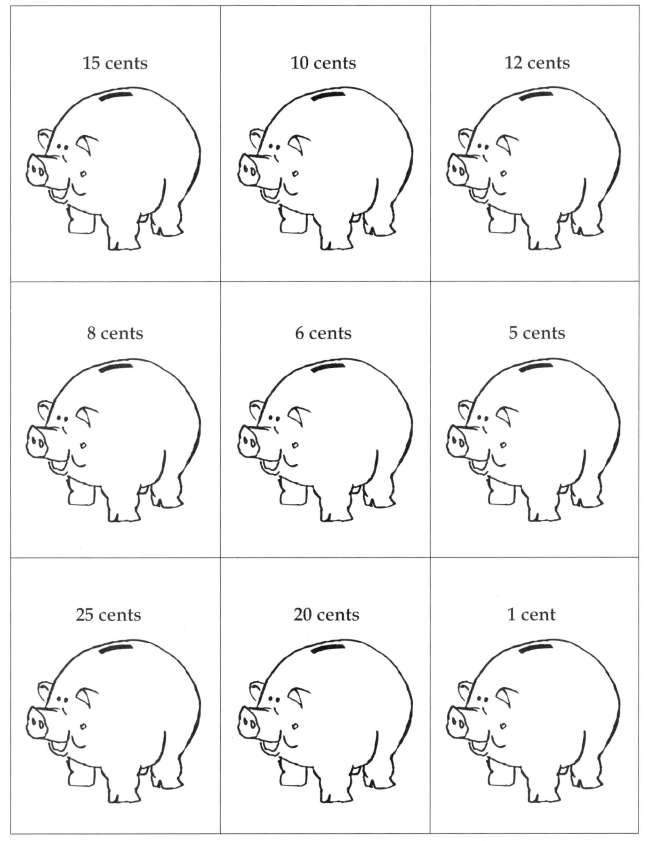

15 cents

10 cents

12 cents

8 cents

6 cents

5 cents

25 cents

20 cents

1 cent

■ The game board can be made more durable by pasting it on oaktag and laminating it.

Pennies	
Nickels	
Dimes	
Quarters	

Appendix E

Student recording sheet for Piggy Bank

Name ______________________ Date ____________

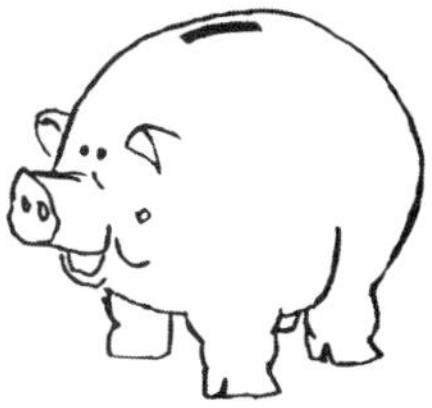

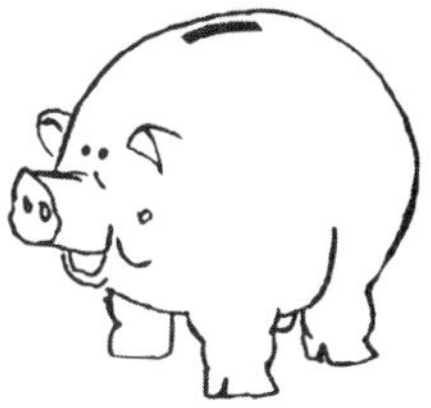

Name ________________ Name ________________

■ Make several copies of this page, glue the pages to oaktag, cut out the "coins" and laminate them.

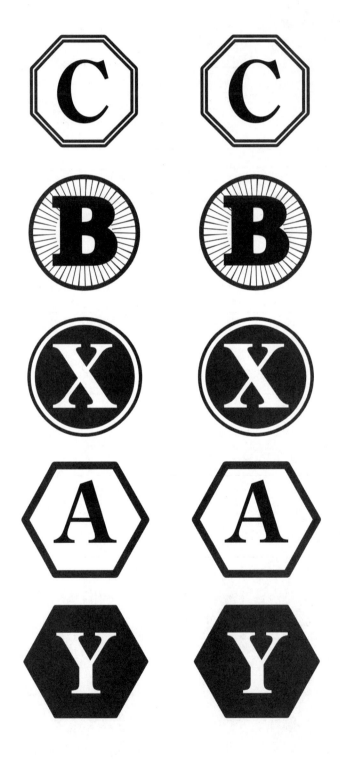

■ The cards can be made more durable by pasting them on oaktag and laminating them.

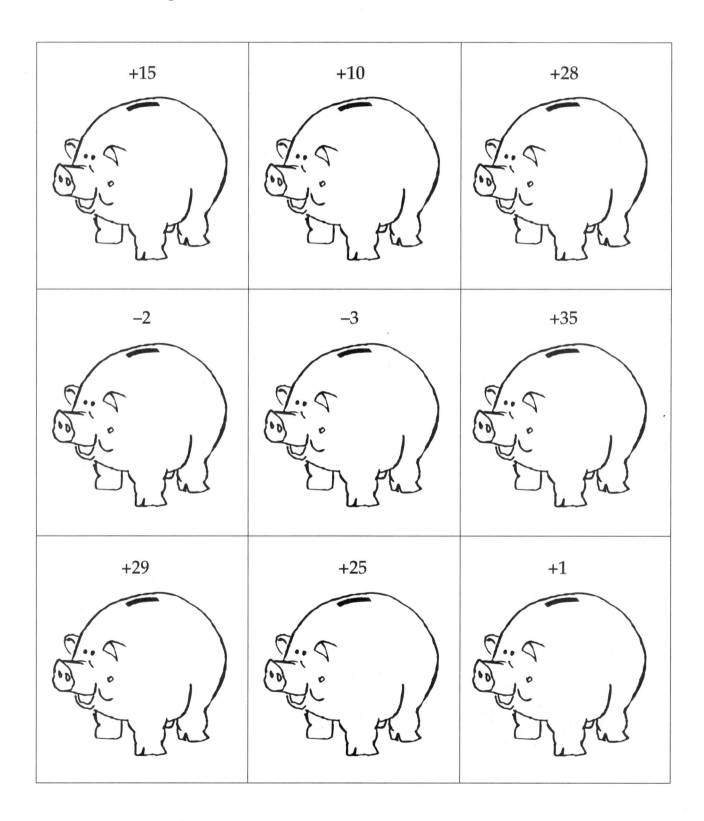

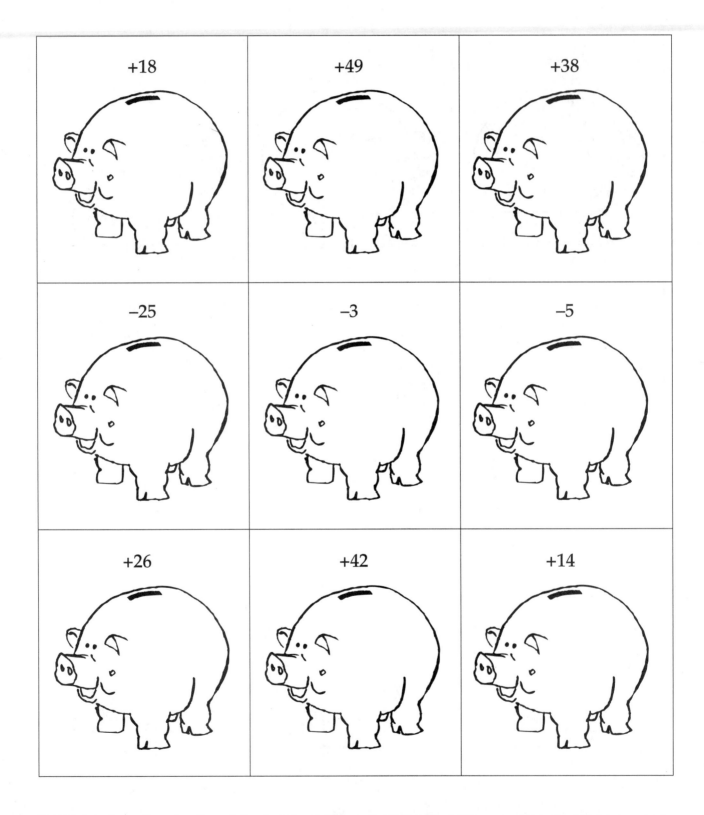

Appendix H

Student recording sheet for Trading for Dimes

Names ______________________________ Date ______________

______________________ ___ ______________________

______________________ ___ ______________________

______________________ ___ ______________________

______________________ ___ ______________________

______________________ ___ ______________________

______________________ ___ ______________________

______________________ ___ ______________________

______________________ ___ ______________________

______________________ ___ ______________________

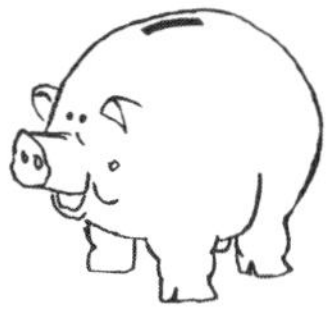

Names _____ Date_____

- Instead of subtracting five, add five and subtract ten. Will this always work?

- Prove it!

Names _____   Date _____

The Mystery of the Foreign Coins

■ Coin a =

Clue: $15 + a = 10 + 5 + 4 + 4$

■ Coin b =

Clue: $8 + 20 + 10 = 10 + 10 + 10 + 7 + b$

Names _____ Date _____

■ Coin x =

Clue: When you are at x on the number line and you take a big jump, you land on 40. If you are at x and you take the same size jump in the other direction, you land on 20.

■ Coin y =

Clue: $y + 5 = 10$
Clue: $y + y + 10 = 5 + 5 + 5 + y$